W9-AMO-484

US SAILING

Basic Cruising

The national standard for quality sailing instruction

4th EDITION • 2013

Acknowledgments

Many people have contributed to *Basic Cruising* in many ways. In addition to the superb team of the design director, designer, illustrators, writers, and photographer, there were many generous volunteers and experts who reviewed, edited, and gave technical advice. Special recognition goes to Rob Johnson, Design Director at *SAIL* magazine, who with great patience and ingenuity assembled all the many pieces from the team and turned them into a book. But none of this could have happened without the support of the Officers and Board of Directors of US Sailing, the Commercial Sailing Committee, the Training Committee, the Safety at Sea Committee, Sail America, sailing schools, and charter companies. We acknowledge and thank them all.

Mark Smith, *Designer*
A lifelong sailor, graphic designer, editor and illustrator, Mark is currently Creative Director for North Sails. Mark was editorial and art director for *Yacht Racing/Cruising* magazine (now *Sailing World*) from 1970-83, editor and publisher of *Sailor* magazine from 1984-86, and editor and art director of *American Sailor* from 1987-89. His works include design and illustration for the *Annapolis Book of Seamanship* by John Rousmaniere, published by Simon and Schuster. Mark lives in Norwalk, CT with his wife Tina and daughters Stephanie, Natalie and Cristina.

Diana Jessie, *Writer*
Diana enjoys racing and cruising, and has completed a 60,000 mile circumnavigation. Thousands have attended her cruising seminars and read her articles in *SAIL, Sailing, Yachting* and *Yachting World*. At present, she lives and works (on a computer in the quarter berth) aboard her 48-foot sloop in San Francisco Bay.

Shimon-Craig Van Collie, *Writer*
A dedicated sailor for over 40 years, Shimon cruised and raced the waters of both the East and West coasts. As a sailing journalist, he covered sailing and boardsailing since 1979. Shimon was a regular contributor to Latitude 38, West Coast editor of *Sailing* magazine and authored the book *Windsurfing: The Call of the Wind*, published in 1992. He died tragically in 2000 of cancer. Sailing has lost a wonderful talent and a wonderful person.

Kim Downing, *Illustrator*
Kim grew up in the Midwest doing two things, sailing and drawing, so it's only natural that his two favorite pastimes should come together in the production of this book. He has been the technical illustrator for *SAIL* magazine since 1988 and is the proprietor of Magazine Art and Design, which provides technical illustrations for books and magazines worldwide. He and his family enjoy cruising and occasional racing on the Great Lakes aboard their 26 foot sailboat.

Rob Eckhardt, *Illustrator*
A graphic design professional, Rob is currently Art Director of *SAIL* magazine and has many years of experience as a designer for advertising agencies, publications and his own business clients. He is a graduate of the Rochester Institute of Technology, Rochester, NY. Rob began sailing dinghies as a youngster and currently enjoys one-design racing and coastal cruising.

Chuck Place, *Photographer*
A professional photographer for seventeen years, Chuck has worked for a wide range of clients, including *National Geographic, Time, Smithsonian, Travel & Leisure* and *SAIL* magazines. Working out of a home base in Santa Barbara, CA, Chuck is able to combine his love for the ocean and images by photographing sailboats, one of his favorite subjects.

David Norton, *Designer*
An avid sailor who grew up racing dinghies on Naraganset Bay and cruising New England waters on his family's Pearson 36, Orion – David is currently the Associate Art Director for Cruising and Sailing World Magazines. David is an award-winning designer, and also Founder of Lemon & Line, a nautically inspired accessories company based in Newport, RI.

Foreword

I was lucky enough to begin sailing the day I was baptized. My childhood summer memories are full of days spent sailing on Lake St. Clair aboard the family's 36-foot classic wooden sailboat. The month of July meant cruising the spectacular North Channel, where we could sail through granite islands that had been cut out by ancient glaciers. Of course, it seemed perfectly natural that there were hundreds of islands (rocks) that we could swim to and discover and name for ourselves — such great names as "POOL ISLAND," "PEANUT BUTTER ISLAND" and its neighbor "JELLY ISLAND."

Of course, as a child I did not always appreciate the benefits of preparation. Somehow my father had convinced us that sanding the varnish off the 60-foot wooden mast was the easy part and the varnishing was the hard part. So every spring we would give up birthday parties and flute lessons for the "easy" work of sanding.

My parents planned and prepared and saved and took us on a year-long cruise through the Eastern United States and the Bahamas and Caribbean. Through this enlightening experience we realized sailing could take us anywhere in the world. The sailing lifestyle meant freedom.

Since then I have been around the world twice, not to mention the exotic European locales for various regattas.

US Sailing's Basic Cruising is the perfect place to start your preparation for many hours of comfortable, safe and enjoyable boating.

Cruising across the lake or through the Southern Ocean requires planning and trust in your boat and your fellow crew members.

With the right training there are no limits for anyone who wants to expand his or her horizons. Good luck and please ENJOY sailing into the sunsets.

Dawn Riley

Dawn Riley has sailed, raced and lived in many parts of the world. Highlights of her many accomplishments include four America's Cup and two Whitbread (now Volvo Ocean Race) teams. Dawn is the executive director of the Oakcliff Sailing Center, the former president of the Woman's Sports Foundation, serves on the board of US Sailing, and is an advisor to several public service organizations. In her spare time she dreams of cruising again the waters off of New Zealand.

CONTENTS

CONTENTS

The Keelboat Certification Series is based on the US Sailing programs that form the national standard for quality sailing instruction.

PART 1

WELCOME TO CRUISING

Cruising offers sailors a chance to enjoy their friends and family, apply their sailing and seamanship skills and quite literally expand their horizons. Like camping on a mountainside, cruising involves many elements, all of which are important to your safety, comfort and enjoyment.

The graduate of a basic cruising course will have demonstrated the ability to responsibly skipper and crew an auxiliary powered cruising sailboat, during daylight hours, within sight of land in moderate wind and sea conditions.

"With repetition comes good habits, with good habits comes good seamanship, with good seamanship comes security, and with security comes enjoyment."

John Rousmaniere
Author, The Annapolis Book of Seamanship

1 Seamanship

A good sailor knows more than just the mechanics of sail trim and steering, and good seamanship is more than the ability to perform those tasks. Competent cruising sailors know how to handle the boat and sails in a wide range of wind and sea conditions, skills that require practice and experience.

2 Organization and Planning

Good organization and planning promote safety and success. Use checklists. Delegate duties among the crew. Have the proper gear on board before leaving the dock. Create a float plan for your trip. Have back up plans and alternatives in case something unexpected happens.

3 Situational Awareness

While sailing, you need to monitor weather, tides, sea conditions and the movement of other vessels around you. A good sailor knows how to translate and utilize input from the five senses, such as the feel of the wind and the motion of the sea, and how to anticipate potential problems.

4 Safety

Safety afloat prevents accidents. Use the proper equipment for the job. Keep lookouts posted to scan your surroundings. Monitor your electrical, mechanical and other systems for early warning signals. Keep a tidy ship; coiling unused lines, for example, will lessen confusion when something has to be done quickly or under pressure.

5 Teamwork and Communication

Teamwork becomes more important on bigger boats where one person cannot reach everything. The boat's leader (skipper) must communicate effectively in order to maintain the crew's cooperation. Non-verbal techniques, such as hand signals, can be helpful in high winds when it's hard to hear.

6 Anticipation

The sailing environment constantly changes, which requires sailors to be ready to shift gears. Experience will teach you how to anticipate what might happen next, whether it's a change in the wind or a part of the boat that needs attention. Sailors who know what to expect and when to expect it are better equipped than those who don't.

7 Etiquette

Unique customs and certain courtesies have developed over the years in sailing and cruising. The last boat to drop anchor, for example, is the first one to move if the wind changes or current causes two boats to come too close. Minding your manners on the water will enhance your cruising experience.

8 Legal Obligations

Sailboats need to abide by the Navigation Rules. Sailors must also adhere to important federal and state laws and regulations. Oil and plastics, for example, may not be dumped into waters of the United States or offshore. Untreated sewage may not be discharged in lakes or within three miles of the coast. It's against the law to operate a boat while intoxicated.

"For the true boatman, final satisfaction comes with the harmony of thought and action, of anticipation and response, that makes his craft an extension of his will."

-Norris D. Hoyt
Marine Writer

PART 1

PERSONAL GEAR

Your personal comfort can greatly affect your attitude towards sailing and cruising. Wear and use appropriate clothes and gear for the prevailing weather conditions. When cruising, you can be exposed to wind and sun for extended periods, so protect your eyes and skin. The sun's damaging ultraviolet rays penetrate clouds and bounce off the water, so use a sunscreen with a Sun Protection Factor (SPF) of 15 or higher.

Using a life jacket, is comparable to wearing seat belts in a car; if you've got one on, it can save your life in an emergency.

Type I Life Jacket   Type II Life Jacket   Type III Life Jacket

The Offshore Life Jacket (Type I) is designed to keep an unconscious person's head face up in moderately heavy seas, but is very bulky. The Near-Shore Buoyant Vest (Type II) is less bulky, less buoyant and less reliable in turning an unconscious person's face up. The vest (Type III) allows the most freedom of movement, both in and out of the water, but is not designed to keep your face out of the water. A popular variation on the Type III vest is the inflatable life vest (Type V), which is worn deflated and inflated in an emergency. The Type V must be worn and be U.S. Coast Guard approved.

Type V Life Jacket   Type IV Life Aid

Hat with visor for sun shielding and improved visibility.

Sunglasses protect your eyes from glare. A keeper cord will safeguard against losing your glasses.

A light, knit cotton shirt with a collar will keep you cool and protect your upper body from sunburn.

Type III Life Jacket

A water-resistant watch is useful for keeping track of time and the boat's progress.

Sailing gloves protect your hands, and the cutaway finger tips permit dexterity for delicate tasks.

Long, loose-fitting pants protect your legs from prolonged exposure to the sun and allow freedom of movement.

A seabag (below left) is usually made of soft, durable, water-resistant fabric so it can be stowed easily. In addition to foul-weather gear, your bag may contain personal items, such as toiletries, spare clothing, sailing gloves, camera and flashlight.

Deck shoes grip even on wet surfaces and protect you from stubbing your toes on winches and blocks.

Permanently attach a whistle and waterproof light (see crew's shoulder in illustration) to your cold-weather jacket in case you're separated from the boat.

A nylon/fleece-lined jacket with a collar will protect you from wind and spray. For even colder conditions, add additional layers, such as a sweater or turtleneck for more warmth.

A safety harness is made of strong webbing with sturdy metal clips. Used properly, it will prevent you from being separated from the boat.

On cold days, full-fingered sailing gloves will keep your hands warm while steering and holding lines.

Foul-weather gear offers resistance to wind and water. The chest-high pants can be worn separately or with a jacket. You should have enough room to move freely and be able to wear warm clothes underneath. Velcro or elastic closures at the ankles and wrists will help keep water out. An attached hood will protect your head and neck.

Long underwear worn under long, loose-fitting pants will keep your legs warm. Your foul-weather pants can be added as another layer if you need them.

FOUL-WEATHER GEAR

Cruising sailors sometimes need protection from high winds, heavy seas and prolonged exposure to chilly weather. Use the layered approach to clothing to adjust for comfort. Wool and modern synthetics like polypropylene provide warmth even when wet. And don't forget to protect your extremities with hats, gloves and warm socks.

Protect the top of your head from heat loss. Wear a waterproof hat with a brim to keep your head dry and warm. A ski cap under your foul-weather jacket hood will help keep you warm as well.

Sea boots provide extra protection for your lower legs. They should be worn only when wearing a life jacket, because these boots impede your movement if you fall overboard.

PART 1

PARTS OF THE HULL

Cruising keelboats differ from daysailing keelboats in a few ways. They are more spacious and equipped with an engine and propeller, wheel steering in some cases, and cooking and sleeping accommodations. Here are some familiar terms plus some new ones.

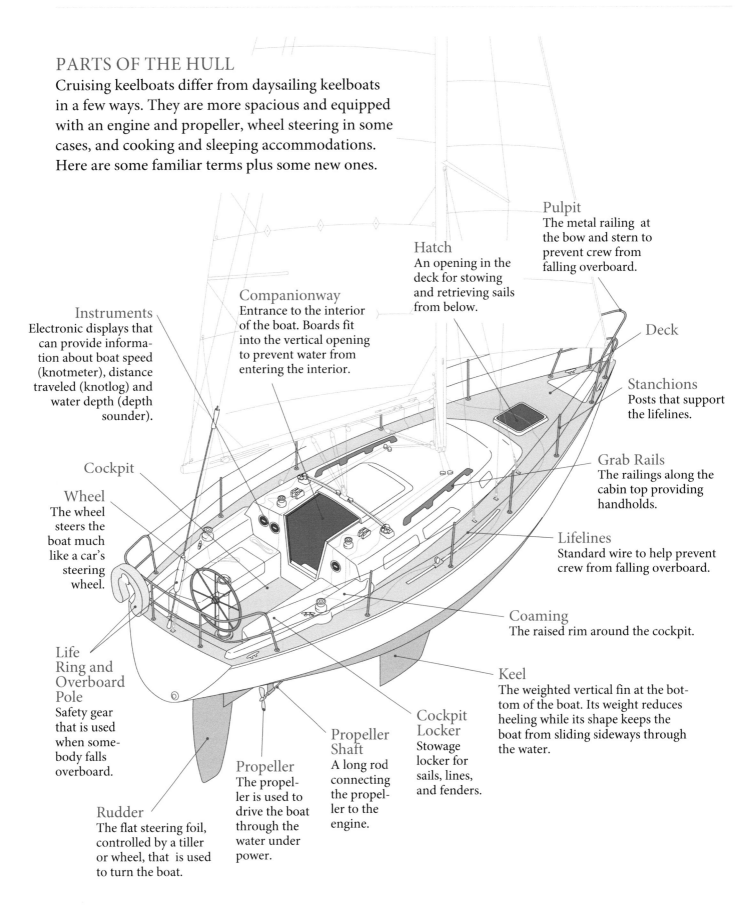

Pulpit
The metal railing at the bow and stern to prevent crew from falling overboard.

Hatch
An opening in the deck for stowing and retrieving sails from below.

Companionway
Entrance to the interior of the boat. Boards fit into the vertical opening to prevent water from entering the interior.

Deck

Stanchions
Posts that support the lifelines.

Instruments
Electronic displays that can provide information about boat speed (knotmeter), distance traveled (knotlog) and water depth (depth sounder).

Grab Rails
The railings along the cabin top providing handholds.

Cockpit

Wheel
The wheel steers the boat much like a car's steering wheel.

Lifelines
Standard wire to help prevent crew from falling overboard.

Coaming
The raised rim around the cockpit.

Life Ring and Overboard Pole
Safety gear that is used when somebody falls overboard.

Keel
The weighted vertical fin at the bottom of the boat. Its weight reduces heeling while its shape keeps the boat from sliding sideways through the water.

Propeller
The propeller is used to drive the boat through the water under power.

Propeller Shaft
A long rod connecting the propeller to the engine.

Cockpit Locker
Stowage locker for sails, lines, and fenders.

Rudder
The flat steering foil, controlled by a tiller or wheel, that is used to turn the boat.

The cabin top may have winches, cleats, and stoppers for sail trim as well as grab rails.

The pedestal includes the wheel for steering the boat, the compass, and the throttle and gear shift controls for the engine.

Compass

Shift controls

Strut

The propeller is attached to a propeller shaft which passes through a stuffng box in the hull. This fitting should be inspected regularly. This propeller shaft also has a vertical support, called a strut.

PARTS OF THE CRUISING RIG

A cruising sailboat rig includes the elements you're familiar with from basic keelboat sailing as well as additional pieces of equipment that add both safety and convenience.

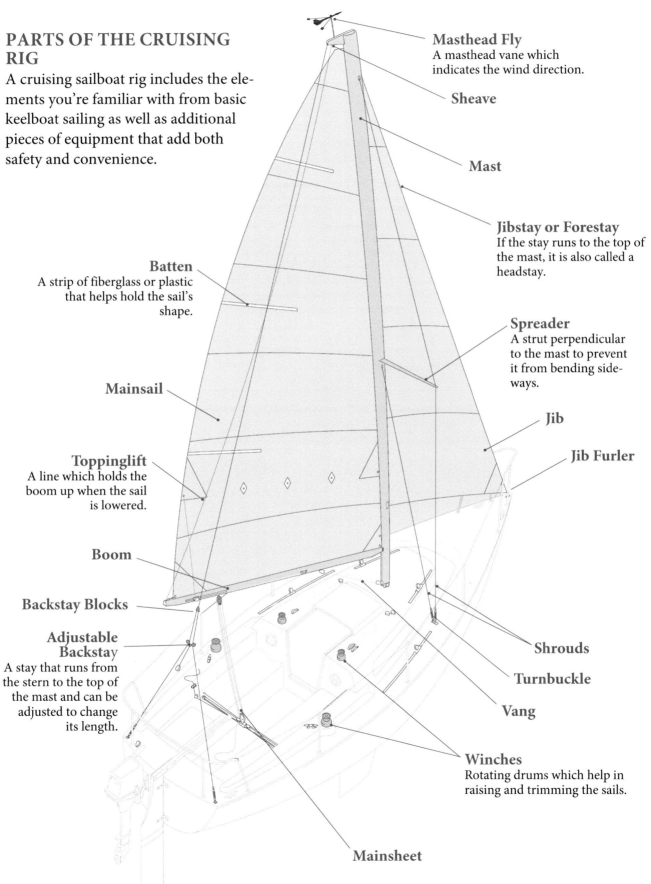

Masthead Fly
A masthead vane which indicates the wind direction.

Sheave

Mast

Jibstay or Forestay
If the stay runs to the top of the mast, it is also called a headstay.

Spreader
A strut perpendicular to the mast to prevent it from bending sideways.

Jib

Jib Furler

Batten
A strip of fiberglass or plastic that helps hold the sail's shape.

Mainsail

Toppinglift
A line which holds the boom up when the sail is lowered.

Boom

Backstay Blocks

Adjustable Backstay
A stay that runs from the stern to the top of the mast and can be adjusted to change its length.

Shrouds

Turnbuckle

Vang

Winches
Rotating drums which help in raising and trimming the sails.

Mainsheet

The shroud length can be adjusted at deck level by a mechanical device called a turnbuckle, which can be tightened or loosened. The turnbuckles are secured with pins, and the tape covering them protects you and the sails from rips or tears.

This is the drum of the roller furling system which allows you to stow the jib by wrapping it around the headstay.

At the masthead, the halyards run over a sheave at the top of the mast and then down to the deck.

PARTS OF THE INTERIOR

The interior of the boat is a compact living area providing the essential comforts of home. Good interior layout is important to cruising comfort.

Forepeak
A storage area in the bow which may contain a chain locker for the anchor.

Forward Cabin
This area contains a vee-berth, a bed for two which narrows at the forward end.

Head
The bathroom is called the head and contains a sink and toilet. Some heads also have showers.

Hanging Locker
A small closet for clothes.

Saloon
This seating area doubles as sleeping and eating spaces. A folding or drop-down table converts this area into a sleeping space.

Settee Berth
This seat also serves as a berth.

Sole
The floor of the cabin. Removable floorboards provide access to the bilge.

Galley
Your on board kitchen includes a gimballed stove, a sink, and icebox or refrigerator. Locker space (cupboards) holds dishes, cookware, utensils and provisions.

Engine Compartment
The engine is located under the galley counter on this boat. Another boat may have the engine behind the companionway steps.

Navigation Station
All equipment pertinent to navigation and weather are stored in this area in or near the chart table.

Quarter Berth
The aft berth is located under the cockpit area adjacent to the navigation station.

IMPORTANT ITEMS

You should always know where to find:

- **Fire extinguishers** - near galley and engine compartment.

- **Bilge pumps** - (manual and electrical) - cockpit, bilge.

- **Seacocks** - head, galley, engine compartment.

- **Master battery** switch and electrical panel - near navigation station.

- **Stove fuel shutoff** - near the stove and at the tank.

- **Life jackets** - various locations.

- **Flares**

This is a view facing forward on a small cruising boat. The table can be lowered to convert into a vee-berth 4.

The saloon 1 is viewed looking toward the forward cabin with the galley sinks and dining area on the port side. Attached to the overhead is a grab rail to use when sailing upwind or in rough conditions.

The chart table 3 opens for stowing charts, rulers, dividers, and other navigation equipment.

A compact galley 2 with sinks, a two-burner stove and lockers. Openings in the countertop access the icebox or refrigerator and other lockers.

Vee-Berth

Head

Galley

Hanging Locker

Settee Berth

The interior of a small cruising boat

POINTS OF SAIL

Sailors have a special vocabulary for the different sailing directions that a boat assumes relative to the wind. Here's your "dictionary" for those terms.

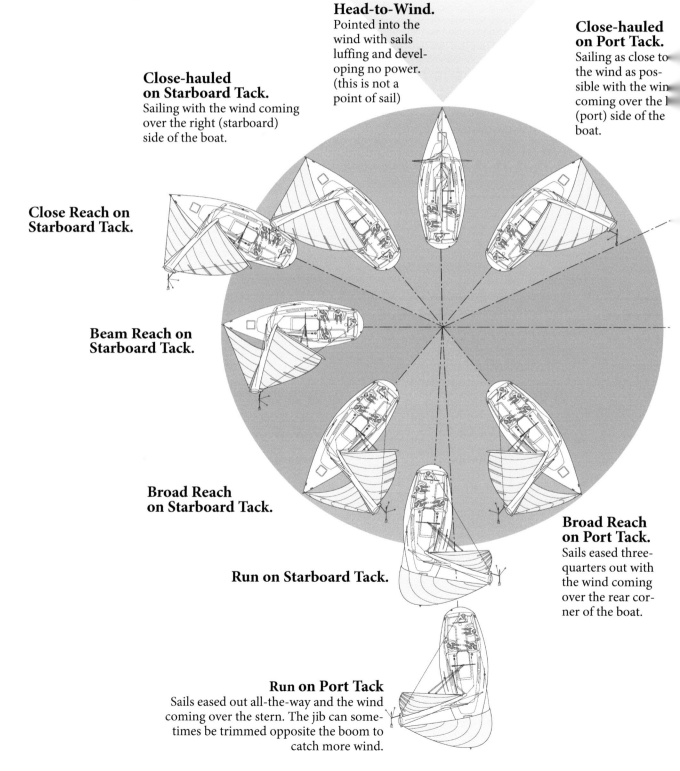

Head-to-Wind. Pointed into the wind with sails luffing and developing no power. (this is not a point of sail)

Close-hauled on Port Tack. Sailing as close to the wind as possible with the win coming over the l (port) side of the boat.

Close-hauled on Starboard Tack. Sailing with the wind coming over the right (starboard) side of the boat.

Close Reach on Starboard Tack.

Beam Reach on Starboard Tack.

Broad Reach on Starboard Tack.

Broad Reach on Port Tack. Sails eased three-quarters out with the wind coming over the rear corner of the boat.

Run on Starboard Tack.

Run on Port Tack Sails eased out all-the-way and the wind coming over the stern. The jib can sometimes be trimmed opposite the boom to catch more wind.

Close Reach on Port Tack.
Sails slightly eased with the wind coming over the port, forward part of the boat.

Beam Reach on Port Tack.
Sails eased halfway out with the wind coming perpendicular to the centerline of the boat.

The masthead fly points to the direction of the wind relative to the boat's heading.

This wind instrument provides a deck-level readout of wind direction and speed.

PART 1

SAILBOAT DYNAMICS

A sailboat is a wonderful combination of balancing forces. One of the most important is the sideways force resulting from the wind acting on the sails and rig. Opposing this force is the sideways resistance to the water offered by the keel and underwater part of the hull. (See illustration to the right.)

These same two forces affect the boat's course. When the point of the force on the sails (Center of Effort or CE) matches the point of the force on the boat's underbody (Center of Lateral Resistance or CLR), the boat moves forward in a straight line. When these focal points shift forward or back, the boat wants to turn. (See illustrations to the right.) You can actually steer the boat with the sails alone. Try it!

✶ For a complete introduction to sailing and sail trim, see US Sailing's Basic Keelboat book.

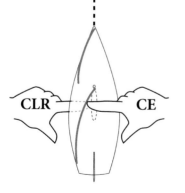

Balanced
The opposing forces of wind (CE) and water (CLR) are balanced and the boat moves forward.

Heading Down
When the mainsail is luffed, the CE moves forward and forces the bow away from the wind. To resist the boat's turning away from the wind, the helmsman counteracts by steering toward the wind (lee helm) enough to maintain a straight course.

Heading Up
When the jib is luffed, the CE moves backward and forces the bow toward the wind. To resist the boat's turning toward the wind, the helmsman counteracts by steering away from the wind (weather helm) enough to maintain a straight course.

18

APPARENT WIND

The wind you feel on your face while sailing is a combination of the true wind that's blowing across the water and the wind created by the boat's forward motion. The combination of these two winds is called the apparent wind. This is the wind you see indicated by the masthead fly and the telltales on the shrouds, and to which you adjust your sails.

True Wind.
If your boat was stationary on the water, the only wind you would feel would be the true wind.

True Wind

Wind Created by Boat's Motion.
Like riding a bicycle or a car, your movement creates a breeze that comes from directly in front.

Apparent Wind

True Wind

Apparent Wind.
The combination of true wind and wind created by the boat's motion is the apparent wind.

GETTING THERE AND RETURNING

Cruising on a sailboat usually means sailing to a destination and returning to your home port. Depending on your destination, you may sail long stretches toward the wind, across the wind or with the wind. At times you will tack or jibe to avoid hazards or to take advantage of wind shifts or favorable currents.

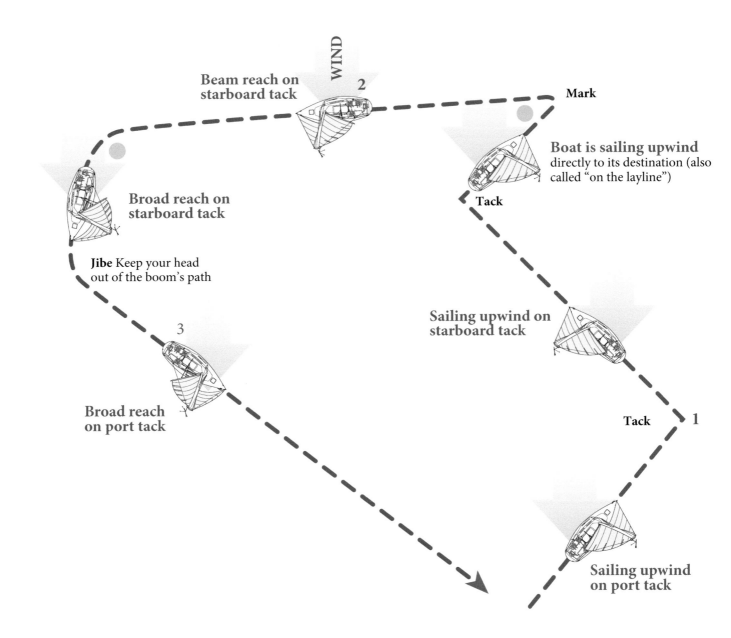

Beam reach on starboard tack

WIND

2

Mark

Broad reach on starboard tack

Boat is sailing upwind directly to its destination (also called "on the layline")

Tack

Jibe Keep your head out of the boom's path

3

Sailing upwind on starboard tack

Broad reach on port tack

Tack **1**

Sailing upwind on port tack

Getting There and Returning

The short cruise shown on the chart uses the following basic sailing maneuvers: **1** leaving West Harbor, sail upwind to the buoy marking Intrepid Rock, tacking twice to pass between the buoys off Pulpit Rock and Flat Hammock; **2** then sail across the wind on a beam reach around Seaflower Reef; **3** return to West Harbor sailing downwind and jibing to pass between South Dumpling and the bell buoy off North Hill. You can plan trips and keep track of your progress by using a chart.

THE ENGINE

Cruising boats are equipped with auxiliary engines, which drive the boat by means of a propeller. Boats usually motor along with sails down, but they can "motorsail" with the mainsail up. When powering, remember that a line in the water can wrap around the propeller, disabling the engine. *Make a habit of checking lines before starting the engine!*

Engine controls are located close to the steering station so the helmsman can operate the throttle and gear shift.

The turning propeller moves the boat. The path of the propeller moving through the water resembles a spiral like a giant corkscrew.

When the engine is in forward gear, the propeller rotates and drives the boat forward.

When the engine is shifted into reverse, the propeller turns in the opposite direction driving the boat backward.

PROPELLER TYPES

Most boats have propellers with fixed blades, but some blades may fold or swivel.

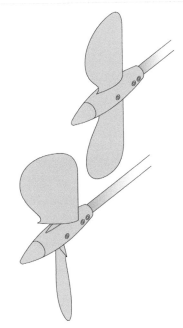

Fixed propellers can be 2 or 3 bladed, create drag when sailing, and are inefficient in reverse.

Folding propellers close when under sail to reduce water resistance. When the engine is running and put in gear, the blades will open.

Feathering propellers have blades that swivel into the working position when the engine is put in gear. When not in use, the blades align with the water flow to reduce drag.

Pull starter

Throttle
Turn throttle grip to control your speed

Gear lever
Put gear lever in neutral, forward or reverse to control your direction

R - N - F

Kill switch
Stops the motor

Fuel line

Kill cord
Stops the motor

Cooling water outlet
Verifies water circulation

Outboard Motors
Smaller cruising boats use outboard motors mounted on a bracket. A portable tank holds the fuel.

Water intake
Allows water to cool the motor

Choke
Open choke slightly when starting the motor

PART 2

ENGINE SYSTEMS

There are several types of auxiliary power used in sailboats including outboard motors, and diesel or gasoline engines. Because diesel engines are mainly safer, they are found in many cruising boats with inboard power. Gasoline fumes can collect in the bilge and explode when ignited, whereas diesel fumes are not explosive.

Engines require several ingredients to operate.

- Fuel carried in clean tanks and kept clean by filters.

- Oil to lubricate the engine.

- Coolant and cooling water to prevent overheating.

- Fresh air circulating through vents and cleaned by filters.

- A charged starting battery to activate the starter motor.

1 **Fuel tank fill** with a cap is marked "fuel" where fuel can be pumped into the tank.

2 **Fuel tank** is equipped with a vent to allow air to escape outside the boat when filling the tank.

3 **Raw-water intake** system provides seawater to mix with the exhaust gases to cool and expel them from the boat through the exhaust system.

4 **Seacock** allows raw-water to flow in.

5 **Raw-water strainer filter** collects debris from the raw-water .

6 **Lift can** combines raw-water with exhaust gases to cool engine exhaust.

7 **Anti-siphon loop** and drain tube break the suction so water can't flow back into the engine.

8 **Exhaust outlet** should be checked for water flow from the cooling system. If there is no water, turn off the engine immediately and check raw-water intake system. Check whether seacock is open and filter is clean.

9 **Alternator** generates electricity to charge the batteries.

10 **Batteries** provide the electricity for lights, instruments, and starting the engine.

11 **Fuel filter** collects impurities.

INBOARD STARTING CHECKLIST

- Complete the engine inspection on following page.

- Turn battery switch to ON position.

- Start engine blower (if gasoline).

- Set engine stop control (kill lever) to the operate position.

- Put gear lever in neutral; throttle slightly open.

- Preheat (if necessary) and start engine.

- Check exhaust outlet for water within 30 seconds of starting.

ENGINE INSPECTION

Regularly look for wear and changes in the engine condition. Visual inspection tells you about each of the systems.

ENGINE INSPECTION CHECKLIST

- Inspect the engine and compartment for signs of fluid leaks & changes since the last inspection.
- Confirm that the raw water intake seacock is open.
- Check engine oil before each trip. Diesel engine oil is normally a sooty black color. Add oil if necessary and take note of how much is added.
- Check engine coolant level. If there is a plastic reservoir, check there. Otherwise check the reservoir on the engine. This should be done when the engine is cool.
- Check the belt or belts for adequate tension. Inspect belts for wear or cracks, and the front of the engine for black dust indicating belt wear.
- Transmission fluid should be checked periodically. Ideally, the engine should be off but still warm when checked. Some marine transmissions use automatic transmission fluid, or others use motor oil. Confirm which is needed before adding fluid.
- The raw water strainer should ideally be checked daily. Close the intake seacock before opening the strainer, and be certain to open it again when finished.

Fueling
Make sure diesel is added only through the deck plate marked "fuel" or "diesel" and there are no open flames (check galley stove) or smoking in the area. Monitor the fuel flow continuously and wipe up any fuel spilled on deck. Do not hose spilled fuel overboard. Secure the deck plate when finished.

Checking gauges
When the engine is running, don't forget to check the oil pressure and water temperature gauges periodically. Some boats have alarm lights and buzzers to warn you if dangerous conditions exist.

Starter
Throttle
Gear lever
Choke

OUTBOARD STARTING CHECKLIST

1 Secure tilt control lever in down position.
2 Check for adequate fuel in tank.
3 Check kill cord.
4 Open fuel tank vent.
5 Check that both ends of fuel line are securely attached.
6 Pump bulb until firm.
7 Put gear lever in neutral.
8 Pull choke out.
9 Put throttle in start position.
10 Pull starter.
11 Push choke in after engine starts.
12 Check cooling water outlet.

Seacock
The thru-hull seacock for the raw-water intake must be open.

Raw-water intake
The raw-water intake strainer should be free of grass, plastic and aquatic life that could clog the system.

Cooling water
Remove the cap ONLY when the engine is cool to check cooling fluid level and condition. Check coolant in the highest placed reservoir.

ELECTRICAL SYSTEM

Starting the auxiliary engine and using lights and instruments are dependent upon electricity. Knowing the location of the wiring, how to inspect the battery, and the operation of the battery switch demand little effort and offer great rewards. The electrical system on most boats is 12 volt DC.

The battery switch and a series of labeled switches are located on the electrical control panel. Most cruising boats are equipped with switches for navigation lights and interior lights. Electronic instruments, radios and other equipment may also be listed on the control panel.

Engine block

Battery 1

Battery 2

High Amp Fuse

Volts

Amps

Battery switch

Breaker switches

to lights

to engine & instruments

BATTERY CHECKLIST

1 Locate the batteries and check the fluid levels (unless they are dry/gel).
2 Make sure the batteries are clean with no signs of corrosion.
3 Set battery switch to the position you want (1, 2, or ALL) before starting the engine or turning on lights.
4 Set the battery switch to ALL if you know the batteries are low. This may provide sufficient power to start the engine.
5 Determine if your automatic bilge pump is wired separately from the battery switch.
6 Don't change the position of the battery switch while the engine is running.

Shore power outlets on cruising boats provide electricity for charging the battery.

Don't
• Don't overcharge the batteries. Read manufacturer information.

Do
• Check the manual to see which switches should be left on when leaving the boat.

(Above) The typical cruising boat is wired to carry electricity to the locations in the diagram. Usually, the batteries are located near the engine. One battery is designated for starting the engine and the other is used for the "house" to operate instruments and lights. On the battery switch they are designated as battery one and battery two. The ALL designation means both batteries are on.

FRESH WATER SYSTEM

Boats carry a limited amount of fresh water. Check the quality and quantity of water the tanks hold, because you use it for drinking, cooking and washing. Small boats have a manual pressure system which you pump with your hand or foot to bring water into the sink. Bigger boats have the manual system as well as a pressure system which operates with faucets like the one in your home. Hot water is created by engine heat or by using electricity from a shoreside source.

Larger boats often have a pressure water system (top) with faucets and a manual pump system (bottom) at the same sink.

The manual water pump can be a hand pump or a foot pump. Foot pumps let you use both hands while pumping. Hand pumps let you keep both feet on deck.

There are several deck plates on most boats. A serious mistake is to fill tanks with the wrong liquid. Be sure to locate the proper deck fitting. The filler cap is threaded and screws into the deck plate.

Sumps

The sump is a cavity or tank in the bilge into which water drains. Boats with showers usually have sumps, which are emptied overboard by a sump pump. The sump needs to be inspected and cleaned regularly because debris and hair will clog the pump intake.

In the boat above, there is a water tank under the starboard settee. Before sailing, locate the deck plate and places where water is used on board.

FRESH WATER CHECKLIST

1 Run the water hose for 30 seconds to clear debris before filling.
2 Taste the water to check quality.
3 Check the deck plate to see it's labeled "water" before filling.
4 After filling, tighten deck plate securely so the water tank is not contaminated by seawater or water used to clean the deck.
5 If the pressure water pump is running constantly, check the faucets and system for leaks and check the water tank. The pump may run continuously and burn out if the water tank is empty.

VHF RADIO

A VHF radio provides local marine weather forecasts, communication with nearby boats and marinas, and access to emergency assistance. The VHF radio is capable of line-of-sight transmission.

The console mounted VHF radio uses the boat's battery for power and has an installed antenna, which gives it greater range than the hand-held model (below). Adjust the squelch control by turning it up just enough to eliminate the cracking sound.

NOTE: For best results, stand clear of the shrouds and mast, and have a fully charged battery pack. Remember to turn off the power when not in use.

Radio Communication Basics

- Use only those channels identified for recreational boating.
- Radio waves are public and shared. Speak clearly, be brief and be polite.
- Always give way to any vessel calling in an emergency.
- When making a call, identify the boat you're calling, then identify yourself, using the boat's name and/or call sign (a call sign is the number assigned by the FCC in the Ship's Station License). EXAMPLE: "Squeaker, Squeaker, Squeaker, this is Cat's Paw. Over."
- When making a life-threatening emergency "Mayday" call, remember the three W's: WHO you are, WHERE you are, and WHAT is your type of distress, situation and seaworthiness. When calling, repeat "May day" and your boat's name or call sign three times and then repeat. EXAMPLE:"Mayday, Mayday, Mayday, this is Squeaker, Squeaker, Squeaker. Mayday, Mayday, Mayday, this is Squeaker, Squeaker, Squeaker. We are half a mile north west of Pt. Sur. We have lost our mast and rudder and cannot start engine. I have two severely injured crew. There are three people on board, hull is okay, but no steerage or power. This is Squeaker. Over."
- If the emergency is not life-threatening, but is urgent, use "Pan-Pan, Pan-Pan, Pan-Pan" instead of "Mayday, Mayday, Mayday." If it's a warning, use "Securite, Securite, Securite."
- "Over" indicates that you have ended your transmission and expect a response from the other person.
- "Out" indicates that the transmission is ended and no response is expected.

Channel Designations

WX1, WX2, WX3, etc - Weather - Provide continuous local marine weather forecasts, including storm warnings and watches.

09 - Used for communication with other vessels, marinas and port captains. Also, an alternative hailing channel in areas where channel 16 is congested. It is NOT an emergency channel.

13 - Bridge to Bridge Communication - Reserved for communication between commercial vessels or a recreational and commercial vessels.

16 - EMERGENCY/Hailing - Used for emergency calls or calling other vessels and land bases. Upon receiving a response, advise the other boat to switch to a non-commercial vessel channel.

68, 69, 71 - Non-Commercial Vessels - Used for communication with other boats, marinas and port captains. Switch to one of these channels after hailing on 16.

72 - Non-Commercial Intership - Used solely for communication with other vessels. Switch to this channel after hailing on 16. There are also local designations for bridge, lock, river and lake navigation. The Coast Guard may have special channels in your area.

STOVES

Stoves on cruising boats are generally available in several sizes and types. Two-burner alcohol stoves may be found on smaller boats while larger boats may have gimballed, propane gas stoves with ovens. Some stoves may have compressed natural gas (CNG) for fuel, but they are limited to use in the U.S.

Small cruising boats often have alcohol stoves which have a cool flame and don't take up much space.

Stove Operation

Propane (above right) gas is efficient and inexpensive but must be used with care. To operate the stove, open the valve at the tank and open the solenoid switch to bring the fuel to the stove. When finished cooking, leave burner lit, turn off the solenoid and turn off the stove/oven. This process clears the fuel line of propane. Always close the valve at the tank when you leave the boat.

Electric stoves are clean and safe. Because they require AC current, the boat must be plugged into shore power, or the generator must be running.

The stove is usually gimballed to stay level regardless of heel.

A solenoid switch is located near the stove to turn the propane on and off. Be sure to turn it off when you have finished cooking.

Propane tanks have a shutoff valve which should be closed when the stove is not in use for a period of time.

Do's & Don'ts

• Always turn off any cooking fuel when the stove is not in use.

• Ignite the match or starter before turning on the propane burner.

• When underway, the stove should be in the gimballed position and locked when at the dock, or anchored.

PART 2

MARINE TOILET AND MSD SYSTEM

The toilet (*head*) is part of the Marine Sanitation Device (*MSD*). Proper use and regular inspection of the entire system is essential to your cruising comfort. Always explain the operation of the head to your crew to avoid unpleasant mistakes. The head is connected to a holding tank because Federal Regulations prohibit pumping waste overboard, unless you are more than three miles offshore in the ocean. Raw-water comes into the head for flushing and the discharge flows into the holding tank by using the manual double action pump. Some boats use fresh water from the boat's tanks for flushing. The holding tank can be emptied at pumpout stations frequently located at marinas.

Deck waste discharge

Pump out hose

Overboard
waste
discharge
seacock

Holding tank vent

Vent hose

Marine head

Overboard
waste hose

Water
intake
hose

Water intake
seacock

Head
discharge
hose

Macerator pump

Holding
tank

Hose connections
should have double
hose clamps

Small cruising boats may have a portable head which has a built-in holding tank. The whole unit is carried off the boat to be emptied.

Note: All seacocks should have a tapered softwood plug attached

HEAD OPERATION CHECKLIST

- Open raw-water (seawater) seacock.
- Open valve to holding tank.
- Engage hand or foot lever and pump a small amount of water into bowl before using.
- Engage hand or foot lever to flush, and pump until bowl is clear. Then pump additional strokes to make sure the discharge line is clear.
- Release hand or foot lever and pump bowl dry.
- Close all valves and seacocks after use.

Do's and Don'ts

- Never pump a head with the valves or seacock closed. If this happens, you will feel resistance while pumping. Stop immediately and check valves and seacock.

- Don't put anything in the head except a small amount of toilet paper or something that has been swallowed first.

- Leave the bowl and toilet clean for the next person.

- Close the lid after using so it does not slam shut underway.

BILGE SYSTEM

Never let the bilge be "out of sight, out of mind." A regular visual inspection of the bilge should become a habit. You will quickly learn what is normal water in the bilge - rain water coming down the mast, ice box drainage and the drip from the stuffing box - and recognize water that indicates a problem. Check the bilge regularly.

All boats should have a manual bilge pump which can be operated on deck. Be sure that you can access the handle and that the pump is operating before sailing.

CHECKLIST

1 Locate bilge pump handles for manually-operated systems and switches for electric pumps.
2 Check the bilge pump switch at the electrical control panel and the bilge alarm. Automatic bilge pumps are generally not wired through the battery switch so they are active even when the boat is unattended.
3 Check all bilge pump intake screens to be sure they are free of debris.
4 Inspect each through-hull fitting for a working valve.
5 Look for wooden plugs at each through-hull fitting.
6 Pump the bilge before departure.

Each through-hull fitting should be clearly labeled identifying its use. There should be a wooden plug at each through-hull fitting that can be used in emergencies.

Ralph Naranjo photo

Tips

• For salt water sailors, taste the water in the bilge if you aren't sure whether it is coming from a leak in the fresh water tank.
• If an electric bilge pump is set on automatic, it can run your battery down pumping water from an undetected leak. An automatic pump might have a counter, similar to an hour meter.
• A water alarm may also be installed in the bilge.

A screen on the bilge pump intake will clog with debris. Inspect and clean it regularly.

Note: It's illegal to pump oil or fuel overboard.

PART 2

SAIL CONTROLS

The running rigging, which includes the sheets and halyards and their blocks, controls and adjusts the sails. The running rigging also includes the sail shaping controls such as the outhaul and boom vang.

Leech Line
An adjustable cord inside the back edge of the sail which prevents the sail from fluttering in strong winds.

Toppinglift
A line which holds the boom up when the sail is lowered.

Shackle
A fastener used to secure lines, sails and fittings.

Mainsheet
The line used to adjust the trim of the mainsail.

Adjustable Backstay
A backstay whose legnth can be changed to bend the mast and control sail shape.

Reefing Line
A line which pulls the lower part of t mainsail down to the boom in order reduce sail area in heavy winds.

Cleats
Devices which hold a line under load.

Traveler
A system that allows you to control the sheeting point of the mainsail.

Halyard
The line which raises and lowers the sails.

Cunningham
A line which controls the tension on the luff edge of the mainsail and affects the shape of the sail.

Outhaul
A line which pulls the clew of the sail out along the boom and affects sail shape.

Boom Vang
A block and tackle or adjustable hydraulic tube which holds the boom down and controls the tension on leech of the main sail.

Jib Fairlead
A fitting which leads the jib sheet back to the cockpit.

Halyards can be led to special cleats called line stoppers (clutches), which can be released fairly easily under load.

A self-tailing winch has a special fitting at the top that grabs the line while you turn the winch handle.

A winch is a revolving drum which helps pull in and hold sheets and halyards. The friction of the line on the drum reduces the pull you feel as you trim. A winch handle gives you more mechanical advantage for lines under heavy load.

Jib sheets are led to the deck, where they pass through a jib fairlead. Many boats have tracks to slide the fairleads fore and aft for different size jibs and wind conditions.

WEATHER

Newspapers, radio, television, telephone, Internet, and VHF radio forecasts keep sailors informed about predicted wind speed and direction, and storm possibilities.

Weather maps help you predict what kind of weather to expect on the water. High pressure systems (H) usually indicate good, mild weather, while low pressure systems (L) usually are accompanied by a warm or cold front and inclement weather.

WEATHER TIPS

- Check your VHF weather report prior to cruising.

- Create a back-up plan for a change of weather.

- Compare the weather forecast with what is happening around you.

- Realize that gusts may be higher than broadcast wind velocities.

- Track windshifts, changes in the barometer, wind velocity and cloud cover.

- Talk to other mariners for local knowledge.

Wispy, thin **cirrus clouds** usually mean good weather for the day, but may be a prediction that a change in weather is on the way.

Towering **cumulonimbus clouds**, or "thunderheads" are usually accompanied by severe conditions, including heavy rain and lightning.

Low grey clouds usually bring steady rain.

Cumulus clouds, which are large, white, and fluffy, are often an indicator of good weather.

OBSERVATION	PREDICTION
Sun and clear sky in the morning	Onshore winds (sea breezes) during the day, and offshore winds (land breezes) during the night usually dying in the morning.
Thermal sea breeze	Increasing strength during the day as the land heats up and decreasing or dying at night as the land cools. Expect the wind to veer (shift clockwise) as velocity increases. In some parts of the country, increasing sea breezes will be accompanied by growing cumulus clouds.
Calm, overcast days	Continued calm and overcast.
Cold and warm fronts	Showers or rain, changing air temperature, winds shift direction. Cold fronts usually move faster than warm fronts.
High cirrus clouds	A warm front with rain and changing winds should appear within 12-48 hrs. Clouds will get lower and more dense as the front gets closer.
Cumulus clouds growing taller (cumulonimbus)	Thunderstorms and strong winds.
Dark clouds approaching	Squalls or storm which may include strong winds, heavy rain, or both.

LOCAL WEATHER CONDITIONS

Weather constantly changes. Recognizing the patterns of your local conditions, such as winds that increase every afternoon, makes planning easier. Some other clues about impending weather are changes in wind direction, cloud patterns and falling temperatures.

The barometer measures air pressure and helps predict weather. A rising barometer usually means good weather approaching, and a falling one warns of poor weather.

A VHF radio tuned to a weather channel keeps you informed about changes and emergencies.

A cold front is a mass of colder air overtaking a warmer mass. Cold fronts are more abrupt and create harsher conditions. Squally, windy weather is associated with them.

A warm front is a mass of warmer air overriding a cooler mass of air. Warm fronts are typically more gradual and bring humidity resulting in rain.

PART 3

GETTING READY

It's time to go sailing! Before leaving the dock, however, you need to make your final preparations. The comforts and conveniences of a cruising boat require regular inspections and maintenance. Checking everything over before hoisting sail is a good habit to develop. Make sure everything below is securely stowed. You also need to familiarize yourself with the wind and water conditions that you might encounter.

Boarding
Step aboard your boat where it's closest to the dock, which is usually in the middle. Place your seabag on board first or have someone hand it to you after you're aboard. Use both hands to grab something solid, like the shroud, and step on the boat's rail before swinging your leg over the lifeline.

SAFETY CHECK

Safety gear
Locate the life jackets, safety harnesses and other safety gear on the boat and make sure you know how to use them. Safety equipment should be stowed so it can be reached easily. Overboard rescue gear, such as a life ring, should be accessible and ready for use.

Engine and other operating systems
It's a good idea to have checklists for the boat's operating systems, especially those which involve through-hull fittings and electricity, such as the engine, head, batteries and electronics. One or two assigned crew members can run through these lists to make sure the boat's ready to go.

CHECKING THE SAILING ENVIRONMENT

Become attuned to the sailing environment. Many natural and man-made aids can be used to give you information regarding the wind and sea conditions you can expect as you set sail.

Tides

A dry piling (left) indicates that the tide is rising. A wet piling (right) means that the water level is dropping and the tide falling.

You can "read" the surface of the water. Wind creates waves, which become bigger and steeper as the wind rises. Here you can see the white caps (foam crests) forming on numerous wave tops, which means the wind is blowing about 11 to 16 knots.

A nautical chart provides many helpful details. Familiarize yourself with a chart of the area in which you're going to be sailing before you leave the dock. Pay attention to navigable channels, buoys, lighthouses, and characteristics of the bottom and soundings. Be sure to note hazards you want to avoid, such as shoals, rocks and other underwater obstructions.

WIND SPEED (KNOTS)	SEA AND SAILING CONDITIONS
0-10	Smooth water with small waves. The boat will be easy to handle under full sail.
11-16	Moderate seas with some white caps. If the boat feels overpowered, consider reefing one of the sails for a more comfortable ride.
17-21	Lengthening waves with many white caps and some spray. Boat will become more difficult to manage and you should seriously consider reefing.
22-27	Large waves, many white caps and spray. Boat will need at least one reef in the mainsail and a smaller jib. These conditions require considerable sailing experience. Listen to radio weather reports for small craft advisories.
28-47	Gale conditions. High waves with white caps and foaming waves. This is a good time to stay ashore!

RIGGING THE SAILS

Think of rigging the sails as getting your boat dressed to go sailing. Start by removing the cover on the mainsail and preparing the lines you'll need to hoist and control the sail. Depending on the wind strength, you'll also make a selection for the proper jib. Use your larger jib for lighter winds and a smaller one for medium and heavy winds.

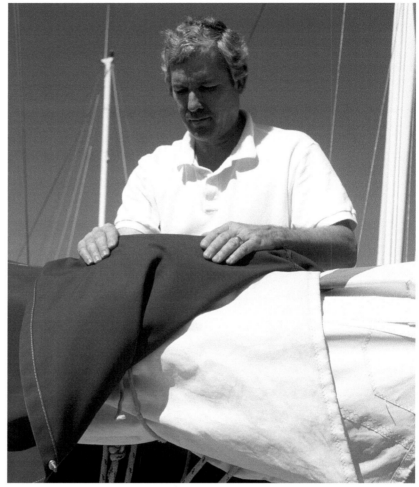

Undo the ties and/or clips that hold the mainsail cover snugly to the boom and mast. Fold or roll the cover up neatly and stow it in a cockpit locker or in the cabin.

Check that the battens are in the mainsail, the reefing lines are adjusted or cleared, and the outhaul is tensioned.

The main halyard is fastened to the head of the sail in a special reinforced hole. Make sure the halyard shackle is closed securely so the mainsail won't fall down once it's raised.

Some jibs are stowed by rolling them around the headstay. You unfurl the sail by pulling the jib sheet and you furl it by pulling on a line attached to a drum at the base of the headstay. Keep tension on the furling line when unrolling the sail to prevent the line from snarling and jamming on the drum.

Choosing a Headsail

The working jib fills the triangle made by the mast, forestay and deck and is good for medium to heavy winds.

A genoa is a large jib that overlaps the mast and gives the boat more power in light to medium winds.

The forward end of each jib sheet ties into the clew of the jib with a bowline knot, which is both strong and easy to release.

The tack of the jib attaches at the base of the forestay. Again, be sure the connection is secure so the sail doesn't come free unexpectedly.

Attach the luff by clipping the special hooks (jib hanks) onto the forestay.

Use a couple of sail ties to wrap the jib into a bundle. Loop the sail ties around a stanchion as well and the sail will lie safely on the deck until you're ready to hoist it. (Don't forget to remove the sail ties first!)

PART 3

WORKING AS A CREW

A sailing crew is a team and you'll enjoy yourselves more if you learn to work together. Like any team, members need to communicate with one another and know their responsibilities. It may take time to work some of these elements out, but you'll be rewarded with a well-sailed boat and a happy crew!

Mainsheet Trimmer

The mainsheet trimmer trims the mainsheet, adjusts the traveler and keeps an eye out for other boats or obstructions that the helmsman may not see.

Big Boat Differences

- Bigger boats accelerate and turn more slowly than small keelboats. They also glide for more distance, which is important if you're trying to land at a dock.

- The loads on sheets and halyards are greater on big boats and require caution when handling.

- Because you're higher off the water, it may not seem like you're going very fast. The increased windage of a larger boat also makes it more susceptible to being blown off course.

- Repairs on a big boat can be very expensive, so be careful!

Jib Trimmers

The jib trimmers trim the jib and take care of the front part of the boat. They also relay information to the helmsman about oncoming traffic or changing winds.

Helmsman Responsibilities

The helmsman steers the boat and tells the crew when the boat is about to tack or jibe. The helmsman reads the compass and determines the boat's course, as well as keeps an eye out for nearby traffic and other obstructions.

COMMUNICATION TIPS

- Pay attention to your surroundings and let each other know about possible danger situations.

- Talk through maneuvers with other members of the crew before you perform them. Make sure everyone on board knows what's going to happen in advance.

- Use hand signals in situations where it's hard to hear or when you're facing forward to perform a maneuver, such as lowering an anchor off the bow.

USING A WINCH

Used properly, winches can be a sailor's best friend. These revolving drums help you pull halyards and trim sheets. The friction of the line on the drum reduces the strain on your hands. At the same time, the pressure on the winch can be very great, so don't get anything caught between the line and the drum such as jewelry, clothing, hair or body parts!

How to load a winch- Put one or two wraps around the winch by passing your hand all the way around the winch clockwise. Pull until the line becomes tight, then add more wraps as necessary to hold against the pull on the line. Insert the handle and crank the handle while pulling on the end of the line.

For better leverage, stand or stoop over the winch, grab the winch handle with two hands and use your upper body to grind.

To ease a line, hold the tail in one hand and push against the wraps on the winch with the palm of your other hand. Release the line slowly, a couple of inches at a time.

Release the line by pulling the wraps up and off the drum.

Dealing with an Override

Sometimes a line will wrap on a winch and jam, often due to a bad lead. Don't panic! You can free a winch in one of several ways.

If the load is light, simply unwrap the line counterclockwise.

If the line is firmly jammed, use another line led to another winch to take the load off. Then unwrap the original line.

If you can't unload the line easily, take the loose tail of the jammed line to another winch, wrap it clockwise and grind the line free.

Removing the winch handle when not in use is good practice.

Winch overrides are a hazard. Don't get your fingers caught in one! Avoid them by only having two turns on the winch until the line becomes tight.

PART 4

STEERING

Sailboats are steered with either a tiller or a wheel, which is connected to the rudder. The rudder turns the boat by directing the water flow. A sharp turn of the rudder slows your forward motion. If you turn the rudder too far, the water flow will stall and your helm (*tiller or wheel*) will feel unresponsive. Regardless of the steering system, you have to be moving through the water in order for the rudder to turn the boat.

Steering in forward
For the rudder to work most effectively, the water must flow past it smoothly. Even a small turn of the rudder changes the direction of the water flow and the boat.

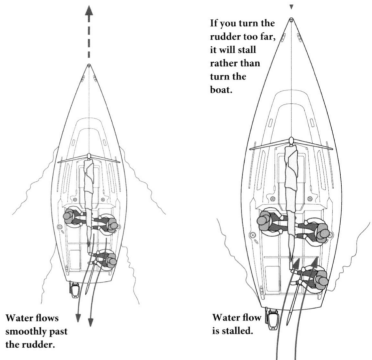

If you turn the rudder too far, it will stall rather than turn the boat.

Water flows smoothly past the rudder.

Water flow is stalled.

Steering in reverse
Use small incremental turns to learn how quickly the boat responds. Be aware that turning in reverse will cause the bow to sweep in a large arc as you move backward.

With a **steering wheel**, turn the wheel in the direction you want to turn just as you would a car.

With a **tiller**, move it opposite to the direction you want to go.

In reverse gear, the rudder will stall at a smaller angle than when going forward.

Water flows smoothly past the rudder.

Water flow is stalled.

WINDAGE

Under power, a boat responds to the wind as it pushes on the hull. The effect of this push (*windage*) can change the way the boat moves, and will vary with the amount and direction of the wind. With practice, you'll learn to compensate for windage.

If your boat is head to wind, the pressure on the bow causes the turn to tighten.

If your boat is stern to wind, the turn will be enlarged.

When the wind pushes on the forward side of the hull, the bow will "fall off" until the boat lies across the wind or farther. To avoid "falling off," steer directly into the wind.

PART 4

STOPPING

Stopping the boat under power is an important step in learning to dock. Always check your reverse gear to make sure it's working. When stopping into the wind, the pressure of the wind on the hull and rig (*windage*) will help slow you down. When stopping with the wind, windage will push the boat, so you may need to increase the reverse throttle and allow more distance to come to a standstill.

Glide Zone
Bigger boats and heavier boats have more forward momentum and coast farther than small boats. The heavier the boat, the more distance you'll coast.

Using reverse gear permits you to stop in much less distance. Always slow the engine and pause briefly in neutral before shifting to reverse gear. Then increase reverse power until the boat stops at the desired spot. Once stopped, put the boat in neutral.

Wind direction will affect your stopping distance.

PROP WALK

Prop walk is the tendency of your boat to turn slightly rather than go in a straight line as this can be significant when backing. The cause is the propeller's direction of rotation. This tendency can be put to good use when you understand which way it moves your boat. You can test your "prop walk" direction by putting the boat in reverse while still tied to the dock. Compare the volume of water flow on both sides of the boat. The stern will move away from the greater flow.

Using Prop Walk

Dock the boat on the side that it "walks" to. Approach the dock slowly in a gentle arc. As you reach the dock, reverse your engine and let the stern "walk" over to the dock.

Using the Outboard Prop

If you have an outboard motor, you can use it to help turn your boat. With both the rudder and motor turned in the same direction, you will be able to make a much tighter turn than if you just turned the rudder. Compare the arcs of the two boats.

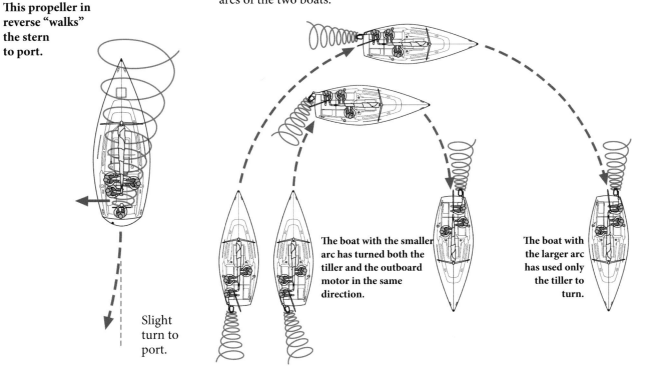

This propeller in reverse "walks" the stern to port.

Slight turn to port.

The boat with the smaller arc has turned both the tiller and the outboard motor in the same direction.

The boat with the larger arc has used only the tiller to turn.

LEAVING THE DOCK

Marinas differ and you will need to know how to leave from a side dock as well as a slip. Discuss how you plan to leave the dock and what each person will do. Before you start the engine or undo lines, check the wind velocity and direction, and the current.

Key Points

- Be sure everyone knows what to do.
- Check that no lines are in the water before starting the engine.
- Get on and off the boat at the shrouds.
- Stow the docklines and fenders after you clear the dock.

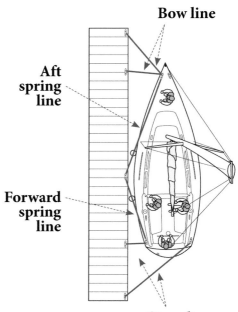

Note: Spring lines refer to the direction they lead **from the boat**. An aft spring line leads aft from the boat. A forward spring line leads forward from the boat.

Stern departure

1 A crew member uncleats the stern line, pushes the stern out and boards at the shrouds, while a second crew member holds onto a shroud and the bow line.

2 The second crew member makes sure the stern is cocked away from the dock before boarding at the shrouds.

3 In reverse gear, the boat is backed away from the dock while crew members coil lines and stow fenders.

46

Bow departure

1 The docklines have been released and a crew member stands on the dock holding onto the boat with the stern line in hand.

2 The crew member then pushes off and steps aboard at the shrouds with stern line in hand.

3 In forward gear, the boat is steered away from the dock in a gentle turn so the stern won't hit the dock, while crew members coil lines and stow fenders.

Backing out of the slip

1 With a crew member at the shrouds holding the bow line in one hand and the shroud in the other, keeping the boat parallel to the dock, the boat is put in reverse gear and begins to back slowly.

2 When the shroud is nearly even with the end of the dock, the crew member steps aboard at the shrouds.

3 When the bow is clear of the dock, continue backing the boat in a gentle arc, then center the helm and shift into forward gear.

HOISTING THE MAIN

When you've found an open space of water with no nearby obstructions, you can hoist your mainsail. Use engine power to maintain steerage. Turn the boat directly into the wind so the sail luffs as it's being hoisted. Leave the running rigging (*mainsheet, cunningham, reefing lines and boom vang*) loose until the sail is fully raised and the halyard cleated. Then adjust the sail controls and trim the sail.

Before attaching the halyard to the head of the mainsail, look up to make sure the line isn't wrapped around anything.

Raise the sail smoothly. If the halyard sticks, stop and correct the problem before proceeding.

Raise the mainsail first with the jib ready to hoist.

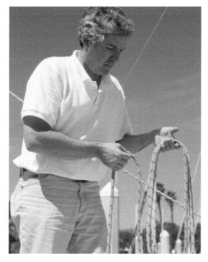

After securing the main halyard, coil the end of the line neatly so it can run freely if you need to lower the sail quickly.

Stow the halyard where you can release it easily.

HOISTING THE JIB

After the mainsail is up and ready, you can continue heading into the wind or turn slightly to one side so the wind partially fills the sail. Leave the jib sheets loose as you hoist. After securing the halyard, trim the sail.

Do's and Don'ts

- Don't grind the halyard up if you meet resistance. Do keep an eye aloft to make sure the sail or halyard isn't stuck or wrapped around anything. Also, make sure you stop when the sail is fully hoisted.

- Stand clear of the boom as the sail is raised. The luffing sail will swing and shake the boom, sometimes vigorously.

- Don't get in the way of hoisting the jib. Do stand clear of the sail and the sheets as the sail goes up and starts to luff.

- Don't turn off the engine until your sails are up and working. At that point, if the auxiliary is a diesel, stop the engine before you turn off the ignition key.

Roller furled jib in stowed position. To unfurl jib, release furling line and pull on leeward jib sheet.

Roller furled jib in sailing position.

If the front part of the jib shows vertical wrinkles (below left), the halyard is too tight. Ease the halyard just enough so that the wrinkles disappear and the front of the sail is smooth (below right).

SAILING UPWIND

Sailing upwind requires some practice. Sails must be trimmed in close to the centerline and the boat steered attentively, while observing the jib telltales. After a while you'll find "the groove" where the boat is making good progress to windward, moving easily through the water, with a comfortable amount of heel.

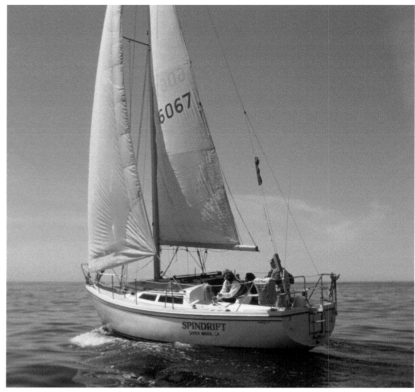

The sails are trimmed all the way in so that the wind flows smoothly off both the main and jib.

On a steering wheel, a piece of tape or line gives you a reference point (the king spoke) for when the rudder is centered. With a slight weather helm, this mark will be positioned slightly off center.

The deck level wind direction readout (apparent wind indicator) gives you the angle of the wind relative to the boat's centerline.

The masthead fly points to the direction from which the wind is blowing. With practice, you'll sense how close you can steer to the wind and stay in the groove.

WORKING TOGETHER

Coordination between the helmsman and crew will help sail the boat upwind faster and more efficiently. Communicate with each other about sail trim and changes in the wind strength and direction.

Jib Trimmers
Trim the jib and let the helmsman know when puffs of wind are coming. Also look out for other boats or obstructions.

Mainsheet Trimmer
Trims the mainsheet. If the boat heels too much, the trimmer eases the mainsheet to get the boat back to a comfortable angle of heel.

Helmsman
Steers a "snake" course upwind, sailing as close to the wind as possible to gain distance to windward and then away from the wind a little to maintain speed. Calls for in and out adjustments in sail trim. If there are only two crewmembers, generally one steers and the other adjusts the sheets.

SAILING DOWNWIND

After sailing upwind, bearing away and sailing downwind is more relaxing and comfortable. The sails must still be trimmed properly relative to the wind direction, but the motion of the boat is usually more gentle. Don't become too relaxed, however! You must still keep an eye out for other boats. If the wind shifts or you sail too far away from the wind, the boat could jibe accidentally, throwing the boom across the cockpit suddenly.

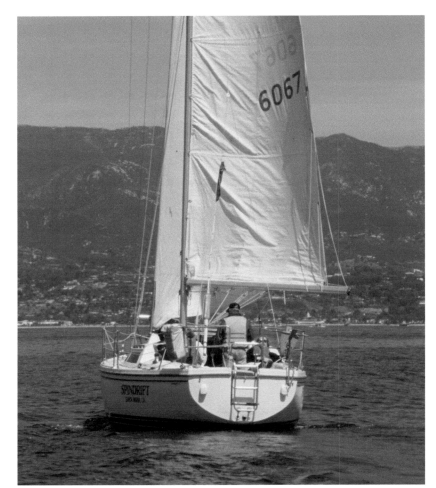

By the Lee

When the wind comes over the same quarter as the boom(sailing by the lee), the boom can swing across the cockpit out of control. If the jib goes limp and starts to cross the boat, this is a warning that you're sailing by the lee. You can prevent an accidental jibe by heading back up toward the wind.

Pull Mode

Sailing across the wind or upwind, the wind flowing along both sides of a sail creates lower pressure on the lee side of the sail, which pulls the boat forward.

Push Mode

On a broad reach and a run, the wind simply pushes against the sails and moves the boat forward.

Jib Trimmers
Trim the jib sheet
so the sail stays
filled with wind.
Keep an eye out
for other boats or
obstructions.

**Mainsheet
Trimmer**
Trims the mainsail.
Warns the helms-
man if the wind goes
behind the main and
the boat is sailing by
the lee.

One or more members of the crew
need to keep a lookout all around
and especially behind the sails for
oncoming or crossing traffic.

Helmsman
Steers the boat in a straight course, watches
for oncoming traffic and monitors the
masthead fly to prevent the boat from
sailing by the lee.

TACKING

Turning the bow of the boat from one side of the No-Go Zone to the other is called tacking. During the tack, the sails cross from one side of the boat to the other. The crew trimming the jib releases the sheet so the sail can pass in front of the mast. The new jib sheet is then pulled in all the way so the boat can sail upwind again.

The boat is ready to tack. One of the jib trimmers prepares to release the sheet holding the jib while the other prepares to pull in the opposite sheet after the jib passes in front of the mast.

4 Helmsman resumes sailing upwind. Crew coils sheets in preparation for another tack.

WIND

WIND

3 Helmsman completes the tack after reaching the edge of the No-Go Zone. Crew pulls in the sheet until the jib stops luffing.

"Tacking" or "Helm's a Lee"

"Ready"

"Ready about"

2 Helmsman announces the tack and turns the boat into the No-Go Zone. Crew releases the working sheet and makes sure the line runs free.

1 Helmsman gives the command that the boat is about to tack. Crew position themselves at the jib sheets before responding, "Ready."

JIBING (GYBING)

The opposite of tacking, jibing turns the stern of the boat through the wind. During a jibe, you should control the boom by sheeting it in before the boat crosses the wind and letting the sheet out quickly afterward. To jibe the jib, take up slack on the new sheet, then simply release the old sheet. Let the sail pass in front of the mast and trim it for the new course.

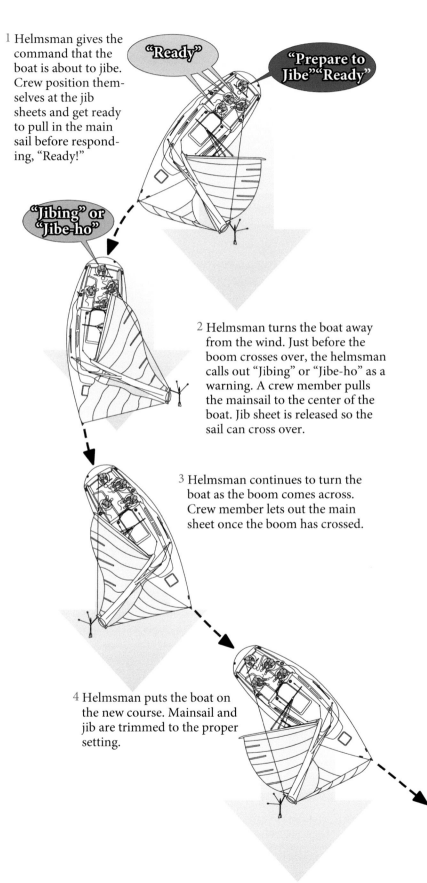

1 Helmsman gives the command that the boat is about to jibe. Crew position themselves at the jib sheets and get ready to pull in the main sail before responding, "Ready!"

"Ready"

"Prepare to Jibe" "Ready"

"Jibing" or "Jibe-ho"

2 Helmsman turns the boat away from the wind. Just before the boom crosses over, the helmsman calls out "Jibing" or "Jibe-ho" as a warning. A crew member pulls the mainsail to the center of the boat. Jib sheet is released so the sail can cross over.

3 Helmsman continues to turn the boat as the boom comes across. Crew member lets out the main sheet once the boom has crossed.

4 Helmsman puts the boat on the new course. Mainsail and jib are trimmed to the proper setting.

PART 4

LOWERING SAILS

Give yourself plenty of room to maneuver as you lower the sails. Make sure that the crew is ready and no lines are trailing in the water that might get caught in the propeller. Start the engine, then slow the boat by turning into the No-Go Zone and let the sails luff. Shift into forward and use the engine to hold the boat into the wind while you take down the sails.

Roll up the jib first. Before lowering the mainsail make sure the toppinglift is in place to support the boom and the traveler is centered and secured. Then lower the sail and fold it, making it fast to the boom.

WIND

Many sailors turn the boat into the wind, the No-Go Zone, to lower the sails. It will cause wear and tear on the jib if it is rolled up on a close reach just before turning into the wind. Another technique is to turn downwind and roll the jib behind the mainsail. Turn the boat back into the wind to lower the main.

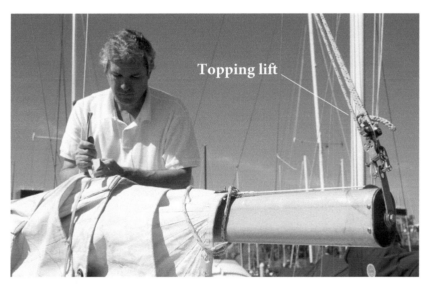

Topping lift

With the topping lift supporting the boom, the mainsail is secured neatly with sail ties.

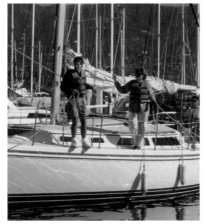

With fenders in place, spring lines, and bow and stern lines coiled in hand, these crew members are ready to step off at the shrouds when the boat comes alongside the dock.

RETURNING TO THE DOCK

Crosswind Docking - leeward side

When the wind is blowing away from the dock, the boat's windage will push you away from the dock. 1 Turn the boat into the wind. 2 About half a boat length from the dock, make a tight turn to bring the boat parallel to the dock. 3 Reverse the engine to stop. Secure bow and stern lines quickly and then secure the spring lines.

Crosswind Docking - windward side

When the wind is blowing onto the dock, the boat's windage will push you onto the dock. 1 Approach the dock at an angle. 2 Turn the boat parallel to the dock about half a boat length away from the dock. 3 Reverse the engine to stop the boat, and use the boat's windage to drift to the dock. Secure the stern line and then the other lines.

Downwind Docking

Docking with the wind requires more distance to stop the boat because windage is pushing the boat forward. 1 Approach the dock at a 45 degree angle. 2 Make a gradual arc, putting the engine in neutral. 3 As you reach the dock, put the engine in reverse and open the throttle briefly to stop the boat. Use the stern line to counteract the windage. Make the stern line fast and then secure the other lines.

Upwind Docking

It's easier to dock into the wind because windage helps to stop the boat. 1 Approach the dock at a 45 degree angle. 2 Make a smooth turn into the wind. 3 Reverse the engine, stopping the boat alongside the dock. Secure the bow line to prevent the boat from drifting backward and then secure the other lines.

RETURNING TO THE SLIP

Bringing the boat into a slip uses many of the same techniques as the previous page. However, you have to judge your stop more precisely to avoid hitting your bow on the dock.

Upwind Slip

1 Make a wide easy turn toward the slip.
2 Put the engine into neutral and let the windage slow the boat, then reverse the engine to stop the boat in the slip.
3 Crew members step onto the dock and secure the bow and stern lines.

Downwind Slip

1 Turn the boat toward the slip. 2 Reverse the engine to stop the boat. 3 Let the windage push the boat into the slip, reversing the engine as needed to control the speed and bring the boat alongside the dock. Crew members step onto the dock using the bow and stern lines to help stop the boat and then make them fast.

Crosswind Slip

1 Turn the boat so that it is parallel to and upwind of the slip. 2 Reverse the engine to slow the boat. 3 Let the windage and momentum glide the boat into the slip, and reverse the engine to stop the boat. Crew members secure the docklines.

Your First Sail

SECURING THE BOAT

The boat can be tied along the side of a slip using single bow and stern lines and spring lines, or it can be secured with two bow lines and two stern lines.

CHECKLIST

- Close seacocks.
- Remove trash and take perishables ashore.
- Turn off all electrical switches and the main battery switch.
- Cover sails or stow them securely.
- Stow winch handles, blocks and lines.
- Plug in shore power.
- Tidy and clean deck.
- Lock companionway.
- Inspect all docklines.
- Check fender placement.

The mainsail will last longer if you use a **sail cover** to protect the sail and reefing lines from ultraviolet rays.

The individual switches and the battery switch should be in the **OFF position**. Check to make sure the automatic bilge pump is on after turning off the battery switch.

Before leaving the boat, make sure the **hatch boards** are in place, and the sliding hatch is secured.

Don't forget to plug in the **shore power** to keep your battery charged. Set the shore power switches as necessary.

ADJUSTING SAIL SHAPE

You can adjust the shape of the sail for different wind conditions. A sail with more draft from front to back gives you more power in light winds. A sail with less draft performs better as the wind builds and you want to depower to keep the boat under control and sailing well.

Ease the cunningham

Ease the backstay

Ease the outhaul

Power-up for Light Wind
A fuller draft adds power.

A fuller sail has more power for light winds.

A flatter sail works better in high winds.

Tighten the backstay

Tighten the outhaul

Tighten the cunningham

Depower for Stronger Winds
A flatter draft reduces power.

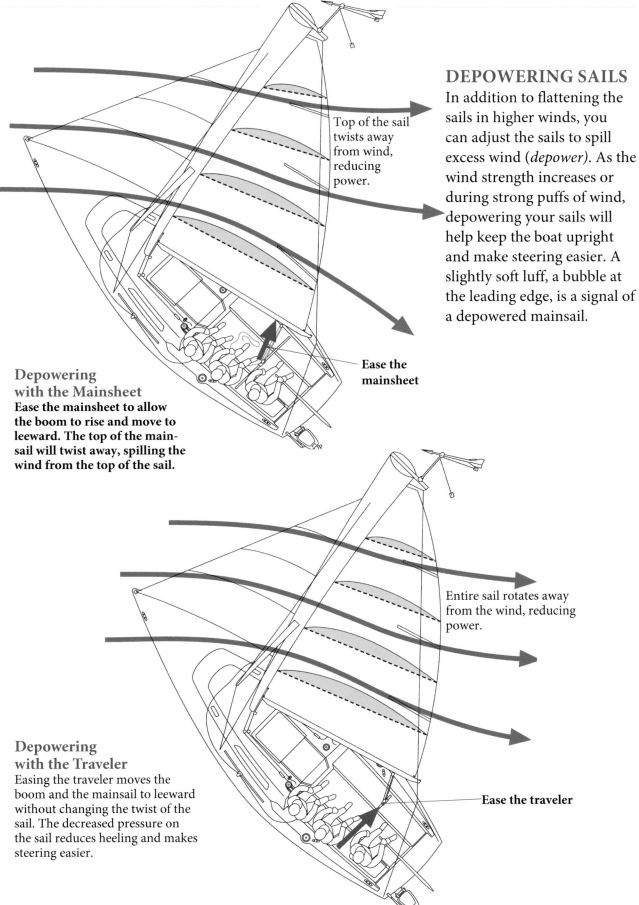

Top of the sail twists away from wind, reducing power.

DEPOWERING SAILS

In addition to flattening the sails in higher winds, you can adjust the sails to spill excess wind (*depower*). As the wind strength increases or during strong puffs of wind, depowering your sails will help keep the boat upright and make steering easier. A slightly soft luff, a bubble at the leading edge, is a signal of a depowered mainsail.

Ease the mainsheet

Depowering with the Mainsheet

Ease the mainsheet to allow the boom to rise and move to leeward. The top of the mainsail will twist away, spilling the wind from the top of the sail.

Entire sail rotates away from the wind, reducing power.

Ease the traveler

Depowering with the Traveler

Easing the traveler moves the boom and the mainsail to leeward without changing the twist of the sail. The decreased pressure on the sail reduces heeling and makes steering easier.

SHORTENING SAIL

Shortening sail is another way to keep your boat in balance and under control when the wind increases. You can choose several options for reducing sail, depending on what's available on your boat, the wind and sea conditions and the direction from which the wind is blowing. Remember, the best time to shorten sail is before your boat becomes overpowered!

Most boats have a system for reefing the mainsail by lowering the sail and tying the lower portion to the boom.

A simple way to shorten sail is to change down to a smaller jib, which will reduce the sideways force on the sails and help keep the boat upright.

Heeling the boat over and fighting the pull on the helm may feel powerful, but the force of the extra wind only pushes the boat sideways and creates drag on the rudder. You'll sail safer and faster with the boat more upright and the helm more balanced by having the right amount of sail for the wind conditions.

When sailing in very strong winds, you can sail with main alone, which will tend to turn the boat into the wind (weather helm) when a puff hits.

One option for downwind sailing is to sail under jib alone. In strong winds on a fractionally rigged boat, beware of placing too much load on the mast at the forestay.

SLAB REEFING

Most boats are set up to reef by lowering the mainsail and tying off the lower section, generally called slab reefing. The procedure is relatively quick and easy (which is why it's also called "jiffy" reefing). Like changing jibs, reefing the main requires that you follow a standard procedure. Reefing is best executed on a close reach.

1 Loosen the mainsheet and boom vang. Support the end of the boom by tensioning the topping lift. Lower the main halyard until the luff cringle can be passed over the hook or horn at the front end of the boom.

2 Retighten and secure the halyard. Start to haul in the reefing line to bring the leech cringle down to the boom.

3 When the leech cringle is tight on the boom, secure the reefing line. Ease the toppinglift, trim the main sheet and readjust the boom vang. Lead a safety line through the leech cringle and tie it around the boom.

Do's & Don'ts

• When reefing in rough conditions, be careful of the swinging boom! If you have to go forward of the mast, wear a life jacket or attach your harness to the boat with a tether.

• Make sure your mainsail luffs fully while you lower the halyard and pull in the reefing line. Keep the jib trimmed so the boat continues moving forward.

• Use reference marks on the main halyard to know how far to drop the sail when reefing.

• To remove the reef, reverse the order of events that you used to shorten sail.

ROLLER FURLING

Most boats have roller furling jibs, which are attached to a rotating rod on the forestay. The main advantage of this system is that you can furl and unfurl the jib without having to go to the foredeck. In high winds and large seas, this can be an important safety factor.

Full jib

Partially furled jib

To furl the jib, uncleat the jib sheet so the sail can luff. Pull the furling line until the sail wraps itself around the headstay and then cleat the line so the sail won't come loose unexpectedly. To unfurl the sail, uncleat the furling line and pull on the leeward jib sheet.

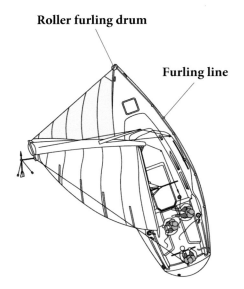

Roller furling drum

Furling line

The furling line is led aft along the side of the boat to a cleat in or near the cockpit. From here, you can control the size of the jib without going forward. In stronger winds, take a turn around a cleat or winch to protect your hands.

If you furl the jib part way and continue sailing, you'll need to move the fitting for the jib sheet (jib fairlead) forward. This will maintain a proper trim angle for your jib sheet.

Do's & Don'ts

- Don't try to furl a trimmed jib. The load on the sail will make the job too hard and you may damage the roller furling equipment.
- Don't rely on a partially furled jib for extremely long periods of time. The sail may not be made for heavy weather reefing.
- In order to avoid overrides on the roller furling drum, don't let the furling line run free when unrolling the jib.
- Bear away to a deep broad reach to blanket jib behind mainsail. This will make furling the jib much easier.

1 Bring the folded sail to the head stay and attach the tack to the bow fitting. Then connect the luff to the headstay, starting with the bottom hanks. You may have to remove the first few hanks of the raised jib to do this.

2 Unfold the new sail. Lower the raised jib and secure it with sail ties or remove it from the deck. Connect the sheets to the new jib.

CHANGING HEADSAILS

Changing headsails, especially in high winds, requires planning. Work with other crew members to get the job done. The wind will want to catch a loose sail on the deck, so make sure you have control of the new jib before it's hoisted and the old jib after it's lowered.

3 Attach the jib halyard to the new jib and make sure it's clear to hoist.

4 Hoist the new jib completely and then trim the sail.

TYPES OF ANCHORS

Anchors hold a boat in position where there are no docks or other places to tie up near shore. Anchors vary in size, shape, weight and materials according to where they're being used and to the preference of the sailors using them. You attach the anchor to your boat by rope or chain, or a combination of both.

Lightweight-type Anchor
A lightweight-type anchor, such as a Danforth, has two large flukes that bury into the bottom. The anchor is light and easy to handle and stow.

Plow-type Anchor
As its name implies, the plow-type anchor digs into the bottom and holds well. This is a good all around anchor, although it is heavier than the lightweight type.

Bruce Anchor
The Bruce anchor has a large, spoon-like blade that buries itself quickly, which makes it especially useful in crowded anchorages.

ANCHOR TYPE	WORKS WELL IN...
Lightweight	sand, mud, clay bottoms
Plow	sand, mud, clay, grass and rocky bottoms
Bruce	sand, mud, clay, grass and rocky bottoms

To set an anchor, get the angle of pull as close to horizontal as you can. This will help dig the anchor's flukes into the bottom. A more vertical angle of pull will prevent the flukes from burying or break the anchor free.

SETTING AN ANCHOR

Since you usually can't see your anchor once it goes overboard, you need to know how it works. Anchors dig into the bottom and hold best when pulled from a low angle. Let out plenty of rode to help set the anchor. You'll feel a solid pull when it buries itself.

Scope

Scope is the ratio of the length of your anchor line (rode) 1 to the depth of the water plus freeboard. 2 Adequate scope varies from 4:1 to 7:1 depending on various factors such as the amount of chain in your rode (less scope) or rough weather (more scope).

Extra protection on the anchor line where it comes on board protects against chafe.

PART 5

ANCHORING DECISIONS

You need to weigh several factors when you're looking for a suitable place to anchor. Some of the information, such as depth of the water, type of bottom and effects of current, can be gleaned from your nautical charts. Use your powers of observation for other considerations, such as protection from wind and waves and how other boats anchored nearby will react to changes in wind and current.

ANCHORING FACTOR	SOLUTION
Depth of water	Water deep enough so boat can swing in a complete circle around the anchor at low tide. Not so deep that you won't have enough anchor line.
Bottom type	Sandy bottoms are always good. Avoid long thick grass and soft mud, as well as underwater cables and moorings.
Protection	Anchor downwind (in the lee) of land or a breakwater and be prepared for a wind shift. Don't anchor near boat traffic.
Room to swing	Make sure your boat can swing a complete circle without hitting anything, such as a dock, breakwater or other boats.
Current	Take into account the direction and strength of the current, which may change while you're anchored.

Anchoring with other boats

Your anchor becomes the center of a circle about which your boat can rotate. Knowing how much anchor line and chain you have out tells you how big that circle will be. Changes in wind or current will cause your boat to swing, so try to anchor near similar types of boats and you'll all swing together.

Boats with deep underbodies sometimes react more to the current than to wind direction while anchored.

Boats with lots of windage react more to wind direction while anchored.

Reactions to Wind and Current

Different types of boats swing differently at anchor. Powerboats and multihulls sit on top of the water and respond more to the wind. Sailboats with low freeboard and deep keels are more sensitive to the water passing underneath the surface, especially in light winds.

PREPARING TO ANCHOR

Before you actually lower the anchor overboard, prepare the boat and the crew. Bring the anchor up on deck and make sure the connections between the anchor and rode are secure. Make sure the bitter end of the anchor rode is attached to a secure point on the boat. Prepare the line so it will run freely. Lead the anchor under the bow pulpit so the anchor line will feed out from the bow through the chock, or prepare to lower from the bow roller. Consult your chart of the area to find the best spot to anchor.

These docks might be a place to find provisions or fuel.

Keep clear of the rocks!

This looks like a good place to anchor: plenty of water and room to swing if the wind or current changes.

Avoid putting down an anchor near cables. Hooking one will ruin your day.

Watch out for the 2-foot shallow area next to the harbor channel. Don't even think of anchoring here!

PART 5

ANCHORING UNDER POWER

While you can anchor under sail, you'll have more control and maneuverability, especially with other boats or obstructions nearby, if you furl sails and use the engine. One or more members of the crew should be at the bow to lower the anchor and send back information to the helmsman.

2 Bring the boat to a stop and lower the anchor over the bow. Make sure everyone stands clear of the rode as it pays out. When the anchor hits bottom, slowly start to back directly down wind or parallel to the boats around you.

1 Approach the anchoring spot slowly. Check the water depth to make sure you won't hit bottom, even if the water level falls with the tide. Prepare to make your final approach either directly up wind or from the direction in which other boats nearby are lying.

3 Let the anchor rode pay out as the boat moves away from the anchor. The person on the bow should indicate (with hand signals if necessary) if the boat needs to be turned to keep the boat going backward in a straight line.

4 Pay out at least five times as much rode as the depth of water at high tide. Once the boat has stopped moving, pay out more rode to achieve the optimum scope ratio.

This is the hand signal for the helmsman to steer to port.

This is the signal for the helmsman to steer to starboard.

If the helmsman should go straight, raise a hand and motion forward.

When it's time to stop, raise a clenched fist.

IS YOUR ANCHOR SECURE?

Once you've lowered the anchor and paid out the rode, how do you know if the anchor's holding? An easy way is to sight two stationary objects, like a tree and a building, that are aligned off the side of your boat. Don't use another anchored boat, however, since it may be swinging and therefore not truly stationary.

If the two objects stay in alignment 1 for several minutes, you're not dragging.

If the two objects drift apart 2 then you're dragging your anchor. Either let out more scope or pull up your anchor and start over again.

RAISING AN ANCHOR

To raise anchor and get underway, reverse the procedure you used to anchor. As the rode's angle of attack becomes more vertical, it should pull the anchor free. If not, tie off the rode and use your engine to change the angle of pull or to break the anchor free.

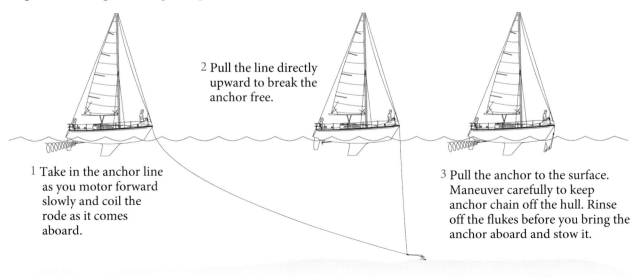

2 Pull the line directly upward to break the anchor free.

1 Take in the anchor line as you motor forward slowly and coil the rode as it comes aboard.

3 Pull the anchor to the surface. Maneuver carefully to keep anchor chain off the hull. Rinse off the flukes before you bring the anchor aboard and stow it.

PART 5

USING SPRING LINES

Muscle power isn't always enough to push the boat from the dock. A spring line works as a lever to turn the boat when you power against it.

Reminders

- Be sure crew members know when and how to release the lines.

- Always take in the spring line quickly to avoid wrapping it on the propeller.

- Retrieve the fenders and stow them and the lines after you clear the dock.

Springing off with the aft spring line

1 With the aft spring line doubled, cast off the bow and stern lines and then the forward spring line. Center the helm and put the engine into slow forward. Then turn the rudder toward the dock to push the stern out.

Springing off with the forward spring line

1 With the forward spring line doubled, cast off the bow and stern lines and then the aft spring line. Center the helm and put the engine into reverse gear with slow throttle.

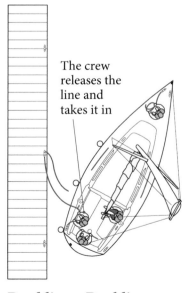

The crew releases the line and takes it in

Doubling a Dockline

Doubling a dockline is a very useful technique that allows you to release the line from aboard the boat as you leave the dock. To double back a line, pass it around the dock cleat and back to the boat.

Note: Pilings often have rope stops which keep the dockline loops from slipping down them. For pilings without stops, you will need to tie the docklines to the pilings.

Docking at a pier with pilings

1 Steer the boat straight between the pilings passing close to the windward one so a crew member can put a stern line loop over the top of the piling. The other end of the line should go to the after deck cleat.

------> 2 The bow swings into the dock from the leverage of the spring line.

--------> 3 Shift into reverse gear and cast off one end of the spring line, pulling it in at the other end. With the helm centered, back up until completely clear of the dock.

------> 2 The stern swings into the dock from the leverage of the spring line.

------> 3 Shift into forward gear and cast off one end of the spring line, pulling it in at the other end. Steer straight out as a sharp turn of the rudder could hit the transom on the dock.

------> 2 A second crew member steps from the boat at the shrouds and passes the bow line around the dock cleat while the first crew member eases out the stern line.

------> 3 Pull the boat back with the stern line to pass a second stern line loop over the leeward piling, while the crew member on the dock adjusts the bow line. The boat is pulled back in and a second bow line is attached.

PART 5

KNOTS

Part of the sailor's skill is using knots to secure lines. Good knots also need to come untied easily so the line can be moved or reused. You only need to learn a handful of knots, however, in order to handle most situations. Practice tying and untying these knots so they'll be second nature when you need them in a real situation.

Bowline

The bowline (BOE-lin) puts a non-slipping loop at the end of a line. The knot becomes more secure under pressure, but remains easy to untie. It is the most commonly used knot on sailboats. Among its many applications, the bowline is used to attach the jib sheets to the clew of the jib.

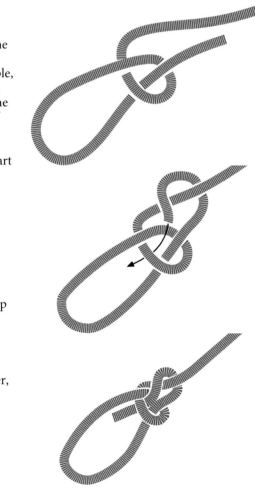

1 To tie a bowline, put a small loop in the line where you want the knot to be, for example, about 18 inches from the end. Make sure the end crosses on top of the standing part of the line. This small loop will end up as part of the knot.

2 Run the end up through the loop you just made, down behind the standing part, back up over the edge of the loop, and down through the loop again.

3 Snug the knot together, making sure the knot holds and the remaining loop does not slip.

Figure-8 Knot
The figure-8 knot looks like its name. It is sometimes called a stopper knot, and is tied on the end of a line to keep the line from slipping through a fitting. Easy to untie, it is commonly used on the ends of the jib sheets in the cockpit.

Square Knot
The square knot is used only for sail lashings. It is not recommended for tying two lines together because it can be difficult to untie.

Sheet Bend
A sheet bend is used to tie two different size lines together. It looks like a bowline, and it is secure and easy to untie.

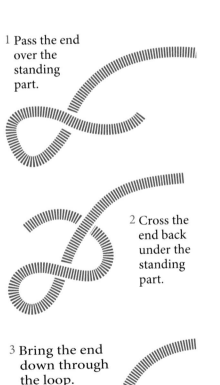

1 Pass the end over the standing part.

2 Cross the end back under the standing part.

3 Bring the end down through the loop. Tighten the knot.

1 Tie a simple overhand knot with the right end going over the left.

2 Tie another simple overhand knot, this time crossing left end over right end.

3 As you tighten the line the knot should be symmetrical.

1 Make a loop at the end of the small line, with the bitter end crossing over on top. Run the larger line up through the loop.

2 Run the larger line down around the standing part of the smaller line, up over the edge of the loop, and down through the loop again.

3 Snug the knot together.

Rolling Hitch

The rolling hitch holds a line to a solid object, like the mast, or takes the strain of another line without slipping. You can tie an extra line to the jib sheet with a rolling hitch, for example, when you need to change the fairlead but don't want to release the sail.

1 Make two loops around the object with the end of the line.

2 To jam the knot, pull the standing end toward the first two loops you made. To slide the knot, pull the standing end toward the third loop.

Clove Hitch

A clove hitch is used to tie a line to an object. It is not a very secure knot. It is very easily untied and, with an extra half-hitch, is commonly used to tie fenders onto lifelines.

1 Wrap a loop of the end around the object.

2 Cross over the standing part and wrap a second loop around the object.

3 Tuck the end under the crossing you just made and tighten.

Round Turn and Two Half-hitches

This knot should use a loop to secure a line to an object.

1 Wrap the end of the line twice around the object.

2 Cross the end over the outside of the standing part.

3 Use the end to tie two half-hitches onto the standing part.

COILING A LINE

A line should not be simply left in a tangled pile, but should always be ready to use or release by leaving it coiled.

When coiling a line, one hand makes a new loop which is fed onto the other hand holding the loops previously coiled. With some lines, it helps to twist the line slightly as you coil to avoid kinks or twists in the line.

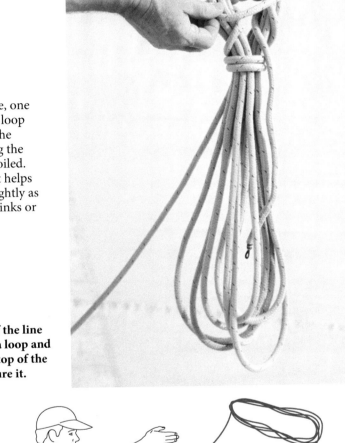

To stow a coiled line, wrap the end of the line around the middle of the coil. Make a loop and pass it through the coil and over the top of the coil pulling the end of the line to secure it.

HEAVING A LINE

When preparing to throw a line, make sure one end is secured on your boat. Hold half of the coil in your throwing hand and the other half in your other hand. Swing and throw the coil underhand, allowing the remainder of the line to run free from your other hand.

PART 6

TIDES AND CURRENTS

Tides are the *vertical* movement of water and are caused primarily by the gravitational pull of the moon on the earth. As the moon rotates around the earth, it "pulls" the earth's water toward it. As the moon moves, so does the water level in most bodies of ocean water. Typically there are two high and two low tides each day on the east and west coasts of the U.S. In the Gulf of Mexico there is usually only one high and one low per day. With a watch, a tide table and a chart you can determine the depth of the water in which you are sailing or anchoring at any given time.

A current is the *horizontal* movement of water and is caused by a river's flow, wind, and ocean movements. The Gulf Stream off the East Coast of the U.S. is a well known ocean current. In coastal area when tides rise, currents *flood*; when tides fall, currents *ebb*. Depending on their direction, these currents can either assist or hinder your progress while sailing. It is important to know the direction and strength of currents. Charts, tide tables, and a watch are helpful in planning your sail.

2 HRS AFTER 'SLACK;FLOOD BEGINS' AT THE RACE

Current is usually weaker in shallow water

Current is usually stronger in deeper water

Current usually runs faster through narrow openings

2 HRS AFTER 'SLACK;EBB BEGINS' AT THE RACE

These photos, taken at the same location, show the difference between high and low tide. Consulting a tide table and a chart will help you avoid running aground during a low tide.

Charts courtesy Reed's Nautical Almanac

The chart above shows tidal currents in Long Island Sound.
Currents are defined by the direction in which the are flowing. The upper chart shows a westerly current. The lower chart shows an easterly current.

Reading Tides and Current

There are a number of indicators on the water and shoreline that will tell you what the tide and currents are doing.

This buoy shows the current stream. You can see that it is leaning in the direction of the current, and the moving water is leaving a wake as it passes the buoy.

A tide table gives you daily information regarding the predicted times of high and low tides and the heights of the tides.

NEWPORT, RI
HIGH & LOW WATER — 41°30'N 71°20'W
CORRECTED FOR DAYLIGHT SAVING TIME: APRIL 2 – OCTOBER 28

	MAY			JUNE			JULY			AUGUST	
Time ft	Time ft		Time ft	Time ft		Time ft	Time ft		Time ft	Time ft	
1 0306 -0.1 M 0936 3.5 1456 4.0 2153 4.0	**16** 0309 -0.8 0939 4.2 Tu 1513 -0.7 2202 4.9	**1** 0345 0.2 Th 1035 3.3 1543 0.3 2249 3.8	**16** 0439 -0.5 F 1651 4.2 2330 4.5	**1** 0357 0.1 Su 1052 3.5 Sa 1603 0.3 2305 3.8	**16** 0502 -0.2 Tu 1136 4.3 1726 0.1 2347 4.1	**1** 0447 -0.0 Tu 1151 3.9 1714 0.3	**16** 0014 3.6 W 0543 0.3 1245 3.3 1825 0.8
2 0335 0.0 Tu 1017 3.3 1530 0.1 2233 3.8	**17** 0401 -0.7 W 1032 4.1 1606 -0.5 2255 4.7	**2** 0420 0.2 Tu 1119 3.2 1622 0.4 2332 3.5	**17** 0530 -0.3 Sa 1749 0.1	**2** 0433 0.1 M 1135 3.5 1646 0.4 2348 3.6	**17** 0546 0.0 M 1820 0.4	**2** 0008 3.6 W 0531 0.0 1241 3.9 1806 0.4	**17** 0105 3.3 F 0623 0.6 Th 1338 3.7 1915 1.0
3 0407 0.1 W 1100 3.2 1605 0.3 2316 3.5	**18** 0453 -0.6 Th 1127 4.0 1702 -0.3 2351 4.4	**3** 0457 0.3 W 1205 3.2 Th 1706 0.5	**18** 0025 4.1 Su 0622 -0.0 1259 4.0 1853 0.3	**3** 0512 0.2 Tu 1221 3.5 M 1733 0.5	**18** 0049 3.7 Tu 1322 3.9 1918 0.7	**3** 0100 3.4 Th 0620 0.1 1337 3.9 1905 0.5	**18** 0159 3.1 F 0708 0.8 1434 3.5 2019 1.2
4 0442 0.2 Th 1145 3.0 1645 0.4	**19** 0549 -0.3 F 1225 3.8 1803 0.0	**4** 0017 3.4 Su 0538 0.3 1253 3.2 1755 0.6	**19** 0121 3.8 M 0716 0.2 1356 3.9 2004 0.6	**4** 0035 3.4 W 0557 0.2 1311 3.6 1826 0.5	**19** 0142 3.4 W 0717 0.5 1417 3.8 2027 0.9	**4** 0200 3.3 F 0703 0.4 1438 4.0 2012 0.6	**19** 0257 2.9 Sa 0803 0.9 1531 3.5 2149 1.2
5 0000 3.3 F 0521 0.4 1233 2.9 1729 0.5	**20** 0049 4.1 Sa 0648 -0.1 1325 3.8 1913 0.3	**5** 0107 3.3 M 0625 0.3 1345 3.2 1851 0.6	**20** 0218 3.5 Tu 0813 0.4 1453 3.8 2124 0.7	**5** 0127 3.3 Th 0646 0.2 1406 3.7 1926 0.5	**20** 0238 3.2 Th 0806 0.7 1513 3.7 2149 1.0	**5** 0304 3.2 Sa 0821 0.6 1540 4.0 2127 0.5	**20** 0355 2.9 Su 1625 3.5 2303 1.1
6 0049 3.1 Sa 0605 0.4 1326 2.9 1819 0.7	**21** 0149 3.8 Su 0752 0.2 M 1425 3.7) 2035 0.4	**6** 0201 3.3 Tu 0717 0.3 1439 3.4 (1953 0.6	**21** 0315 3.3 W 0904 0.6 1548 3.8 2237 0.7	**6** 0225 3.3 F 0742 0.2 1504 3.9 2033 0.5	**21** 0334 3.0 F 0904 0.8 1607 3.7 2259 1.0	**6** 0408 3.5 Su 0932 0.1 1642 4.4 2243 0.3	**21** 0450 3.0 M 1017 0.9 1716 3.6 2344 0.9
7 0143 3.0 Su 0656 0.5 (1919 0.7	**22** 0250 3.5 M 0900 0.3 1524 3.7 2158 0.5	**7** 0259 3.2 W 0814 0.2 1535 3.7 2101 0.5	**22** 0410 3.1 Th 1007 0.6 1641 3.8 2334 0.7	**7** 0326 3.3 Sa 0844 0.1 1602 4.1 2145 0.4	**22** 0429 3.0 Su 1003 0.8 1659 3.7 2349 0.9	**7** 0510 3.7 M 1044 0.0 1740 4.6 2350 0.0	**22** 0541 3.2 Tu 1116 0.8 1804 3.8
8 0240 3.0 M 0752 0.5 1517 3.1 2025 0.6	**23** 0349 3.4 Tu 1004 0.3 1620 3.8 2306 0.4	**8** 0357 3.3 Th 0915 0.1 1630 4.0 2210 0.3	**23** 0502 3.0 F 1056 0.6 1730 3.9	**8** 0428 3.4 Su 0949 0.0 Sa 1700 4.4 2255 0.1	**23** 0521 3.1 Su 1747 3.6	**8** 0607 4.0 Tu 1152 -0.2 1835 4.8	**23** 0017 0.7 W 0627 3.5 1246 0.6 1848 4.0
9 0338 3.1 Tu 0853 0.4 1611 3.4 2135 0.5	**24** 0444 3.3 W 1057 0.3 1711 3.9 2359 0.3	**9** 0454 3.4 F 1017 -0.1 1724 4.4 2315 -0.0	**24** 0019 0.6 Sa 1138 0.5 1816 4.0	**9** 0527 3.7 M 1056 -0.1 Su 1757 4.7	**24** 0028 0.7 M 1147 0.6 1833 4.0	**9** 0047 -0.2 W 0702 4.2 1258 -0.4 1927 4.9	**24** 0048 0.6 Th 0711 3.7 1330 0.4 1930 4.1
10 0433 3.3 W 0954 0.2 1703 3.8 2241 0.2	**25** 0534 3.3 Th 1141 0.3 1759 4.0	**10** 0550 3.7 Sa 1117 -0.3 1817 4.7	**25** 0054 0.6 Su 1217 0.4 1859 4.1	**10** 0000 0.1 M 0624 3.9 1159 -0.3 1851 5.0	**25** 0055 0.6 Tu 1229 0.5 1916 4.1	**10** 0137 -0.4 Th 0753 4.5 O 2017 4.9	**25** 0120 0.2 F 0753 4.0 2011 4.2
11 0526 3.5 Th 1052 -0.1 1753 4.2 2341 -0.0	**26** 0042 0.3 F 0621 3.4 1217 0.3 1843 4.1	**11** 0015 -0.3 Su 0644 3.9 1215 -0.5 1909 5.0	**26** 0123 0.4 M 1254 0.4 1942 4.2	**11** 0058 -0.3 Tu 0718 4.2 1259 -0.5 1944 5.1	**26** 0124 0.5 W 1309 0.4 1958 4.2	**11** 0224 -0.5 F 0842 4.6 1438 -0.5 2105 4.8	**26** 0153 0.0 Sa 1405 0.0 ● 2051 4.2
12 0617 3.7 F 1842 4.5	**27** 0117 0.2 Sa 0705 3.4 1250 0.2 1926 4.2	**12** 0111 -0.3 M 0737 4.2 1312 -0.6 2001 5.1	**27** 0151 0.3 Tu 0805 3.7 1331 0.3 ● 2035 4.2	**12** 0152 -0.5 W 0811 4.4 1357 -0.7 ● 2038 4.2	**27** 0153 0.2 Th 0821 3.7 2035 5.1	**12** 0307 -0.5 Sa 0931 4.7 1526 -0.4 2152 4.6	**27** 0228 -0.1 Su 0914 4.2 2131 4.2
13 0036 -0.5 Sa 0707 3.9 1147 -0.4 1931 4.8	**28** 0146 0.2 Su 0748 3.5 1322 0.2 2007 4.3	**13** 0205 -0.3 Tu 0829 4.2 1407 -0.6 O 2052 5.1	**28** 0220 0.2 W 0847 3.8 1408 0.3 2118 4.2	**13** 0242 -0.6 Th 0903 4.5 1450 -0.7 2126 5.0	**28** 0224 0.1 F 1408 0.2 2116 4.2	**13** 0348 -0.4 Su 1019 4.6 1612 -0.1 2239 4.3	**28** 0304 -0.2 M 0955 4.3 2213 4.0
14 0128 -0.7 Su 0757 4.1 O 2020 5.0	**29** 0214 0.1 M 0830 3.6 1355 0.1 2047 4.1	**14** 0257 -0.2 W 0922 4.2 1501 -0.6 2144 5.0	**29** 0251 0.2 Th 0929 3.9 1445 0.3 2158 4.1	**14** 0330 -0.6 F 0954 4.5 1543 -0.4 2216 4.8	**29** 0257 0.0 Sa 0943 3.9 1505 0.2 2158 4.1	**14** 0427 -0.2 M 1106 4.4 1656 0.1 2326 4.0	**29** 0342 -0.2 Tu 1038 4.3 2257 3.7
15 0219 -0.8 M 0848 4.2 1421 -0.6 2110 5.0	**30** 0243 0.1 Tu 0911 3.5 1430 0.2 2127 4.0	**15** 0348 -0.0 Th 1015 4.3 1555 -0.5 2237 4.8	**30** 0323 0.1 F 1010 3.5 Sa 1545 0.2 2224 3.9	**15** 0417 -0.5 Sa 1045 4.5 1634 -0.2 2306 4.5	**30** 0331 -0.1 Su 1024 3.9 1545 0.2 2238 3.7	**15** 0505 0.1 Tu 1155 4.2 1740 0.5	**30** 0423 -0.2 W 1125 4.2 1657 0.4 2346 3.7
	31 0313 0.1 W 0953 3.4 1505 0.2 2208 3.9				**31** 0407 -0.0 M 1106 3.9 1627 0.3 2321 3.8		**31** 0508 -0.1 Th 1217 4.1 1749 0.6

TIME MERIDIAN 75°W — 0000h is midnight, 1200h is noon.
Heights in feet are referenced to mean lower low water, the chart datum of soundings.

RHODE ISLAND

Table courtesy Reed's Nautical Almanac

Compensating for Current

If you are going to sail across a current you can compensate for the effect it will have on your boat. Instead of steering directly toward your goal, steer for a point upstream, and let the current pull you back to your desired course.

This boat aimed directly for its destination (035 degrees) but was pulled downstream by the current.

035°

020°

CURRENT

This boat steered a course (020 degrees) upstream of its goal and reached its planned destination.

PART 6

NAVIGATION RULES UNDER SAIL

The basic purpose of the Navigation Rules is to avoid collisions. The boat that has right-of-way is the stand-on vessel and should maintain course and speed. The give-way vessel must keep out of the way and should make its change of course obvious and early. It is always a vessel's obligation to avoid collisions even if it has the right-of-way.

Starboard Tack over Port Tack
When sailboats approach on opposite tacks, the boat on starboard tack has the right-of-way and is the stand-on vessel. The port tack boat, or give-way vessel, should change course to pass behind the other boat.

Leeward over Windward
When two sailboats meet on the same tack, the upwind (windward) boat is the give-way vessel and should steer behind the leeward boat, which is the stand-on vessel.

Overtaken over Overtaking
The boat that is doing the passing is the give-way vessel and may pass to either side of the stand-on vessel. The stand-on vessel should hold its course.

Difficulty in Maneuvering
Ships in channels, tugboats with tows, and working commercial fishing vessels may have difficulty maneuvering. For safety and courtesy, you may give-way to these vessels. See pages 115-122 for Navigation Rules.

Sailboats over Powerboats
When sailboats and powerboats meet, the sailboat is the stand-on vessel unless it is overtaking. The powerboat is the give-way vessel because it is more maneuverable.

NAVIGATION RULES UNDER POWER

When your sailboat is propelled by an engine, you are a powerboat. Even when motorsailing, you must comply with the rules for power. Sound signals are exchanged to communicate intended course changes. The prolonged blast is four to six seconds in duration while the short blast is one second to two seconds. Five or more short blasts is the danger signal. When you hear this signal it means a dangerous situation exists or your intended course change is not acceptable.

Overtaking

The passing (overtaking) boat is the give-way vessel and may pass to either side of the stand-on vessel.

NOTE: Traffic separation zones or vessel traffic lanes are reserved for use by large vesels and others with restricted maneuverability. You should stay clear of these zones. If it's necessary to cross a zone, do it at a 90 degree angle (or as close as you can) and as quickly as possible.

WARNING...

Five or more short blasts indicates danger or doubt of a vessel's intentions.

Crossing

When two boats are on an intersecting course, the boat on your starboard side is the stand-on vessel, and you must alter course as the give-way vessel.

Head-on

When two boats approach each other, they should alter course to starboard to pass port side to port side.

PART 6

BASIC NAVIGATION & PILOTING CONCEPTS

Think "navigating and piloting" and most boaters immediately imagine GPS screens and chart plotters because these are the most common sources of access to navigation data. The primary tools, however, are the paper chart and a good pair of eyes. GPS makes using both of these easier, and a plotter in the right hands can render the paper almost redundant, but the navigator has to assume electronics will fail. This chapter deals with the concepts needed to pilot safely in daylight.

The Chart

There are two basic types of charts: paper charts and electronic charts. To use a paper chart all you need is vision and some simple instruments while electronic charts can only be operated through an electronic chart plotter.

Most nautical charts use a Mercator projection to transfer the image of Earth's spherical surface onto a flat piece of paper. The primary advantage of a Mercator chart is that lines of latitude and longitude form an easy-to-use rectangular grid, which allows compass courses to be drawn as a straight line from one place to another.

Paper charts typically show areas of water and adjacent portions of coastline together with information useful for navigation, such as navigation aids (i.e., beacons and buoys), underwater features and landmarks on shore. Symbols and abbreviations are frequently used to convey this information, many of which are largely self-explanatory, but NOS (National Ocean Service) Chart No. 1 is a helpful reference for any you don't find obvious. The title block contains a great deal of important information, including units of soundings (water depths) and heights of land elevations. On this chart soundings are in feet. Other charts may have them in fathoms (1 fathom = 6 feet), fathoms and feet, or meters. If fathoms are used, fathoms with a feet subscript may be used in shallower water. For example, a depth of 4 fathoms and 3 feet would be indicated as 43. If the soundings unit is in meters, the soundings will be indicated in meters and tenths of meters with the tenths shown as a subscript. Thus, 1.3 meters would be 13. Note also the depth contour lines. These are often picked out in colors, making them easy to spot at a glance. If your chart doesn't cover enough ground for the passage you want to make, you might change to one drawn to a larger scale. This will show a wider spread of coastline, but will have less detail. So for safe piloting, you'll probably need both.

Line of longitude   **Line of latitude**

Lines of longitude appear parallel on the chart, but they converge toward the poles (see globe).

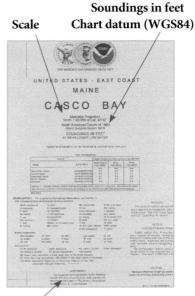

Title block includes chart datum, scale, and measurement units for soundings and heights. Date that the chart was issued along with any corrections are located in bottom left corner. Keep current charts on board and update them with Local Notices to Mariners changes.

The small numbers scattered throughout the water are soundings or depths at low tide (at mean lower low water) at those particular points.

A contour line follows a constant water depth. Areas of shallower waters are indicated in light blue.

Symbols are used to indicate aids to navigation. Red and green diamond shapes indicate buoys.

Types of bottom are indicated, such as mud, sand, grass or rocky, that you can expect when looking for a place to anchor.

Onshore landmarks, such as towers, can be used as navigation references.

A compass rose is printed on every nautical chart.

Position of vessel **Course and speed over ground** **Heading**

Position of cursor

An electronic plotter screen showing a chart zoomed to a usable scale for general piloting.

Electronic charts do the same job as paper, but at first sight they are not as easy to read. This is because of scale. Charts used in plotters (other than PC plotters) come in various formats and are either preinstalled or bought separately on data cards and uploaded to the unit. Once installed into a plotter, they can be read.

PART 6

Any electronic chart contains all the information available within its boundaries, regardless of scale. If all this data were displayed, the chart would be unusable, so the plotter filters it for you. As you zoom in and out for an overview or more details, features appear and disappear. The plotter's default is often to center its view on your vessel, but if you need to see what's happening elsewhere you can move across the chart, then zoom in or out again. This method is the only way of using electronic charts. The more you do it, the easier it becomes, but the watchword is that unless you zoom right in, the chart may be hiding something vital.

GPS Settings
Check the default settings of your GPS and modify them to suit your needs. Here are some settings to consider.
- Datum (WGS84 is standard, but must agree with the datum used for your chart)
- Speed (knots)
- Distance (nautical miles)
- Time (24-hour clock and local time)
- True or Magnetic North
- Latitude & Longitude (degrees, minutes, decimals of minutes)

The lighthouse structure (inset) indicates dangerous surrounding rocks or rip-rap by the greenish brown area around it.

An electronic chart zoomed in tightly – note that there's lots of useful close-in detail, but overview is non-existent.

The same lighthouse shown inset above indicates no rip-rap.

The same chart zoomed out for overview – note the lack of useful detail.

Plotters have menus full of tools but one of the easiest to access is often Declutter. This chart has been decluttered to clarify the overview. However, much vital detail is obscured.

With Declutter switched off, depths and other important data are visible. It is critical never to leave a chart decluttered and to forget you have done so.

84

POSITION

Lines of latitude and longitude (lat/long) are used to define position on a chart. Both latitude and longitude are measured in degrees (°), minutes (') and decimals of minutes, or degrees, minutes and seconds ("). On a chart, minutes and seconds have nothing to do with time, they are simply subdivisions of a degree. 60 minutes equals 1 degree and 60 seconds equals 1 minute. Check to determine whether your chart is using decimals of minutes or seconds. Latitude is measured north or south from the Equator (0°) to the poles (90°) and longitude is measured east or west from the Prime Meridian through Greenwich Observatory in England (0°) to the International Date Line in the Pacific Ocean (180°).

Position on an Electronic Chart. Depending on how you have manipulated the menus, the position of your vessel or the plotter's cursor can generally be read off the data boxes in a chart plotter screen. This is because, with its built-in GPS locator, the plotter already knows the location of anything on the chart it is using.

To plot a position of 41°13.4' North latitude and 71°30.8' West longitude (normally written or read out as 41 13.4N 071 30.8W), locate these positions on the latitude and longitude scales and transfer them by right-angles to the position on the chart. This can be done by any suitable instruments, including a chart protractor, dividers and parallel rulers.

GPS navigation screens vary, but the important thing when plotting is the position (location) of latitude and longitude.

PART 6

DISTANCE

On the Paper Chart. One minute of latitude (NOT longitude) is equal to one nautical mile. This convenient arrangement means that to measure distance, you have only to define it **A** on the chart with your dividers, then carry them over to the latitude scale near a latitude line where you've measured the distance and read off how many minutes and decimals of a minute their spread covers. In this case, the distance **A** between the charted features is 3.4 miles (3.4 minutes of latitude).

On the Plotter. If you search the menus, you'll find that many plotters have electronic dividers that do the same job as the real thing on a paper chart. This plotter calls them a ruler. Note the distance (16.501 nm) and bearing (294° M) readout on the line from A to B. Often, the distance you really want is how far something is from the yacht. This is readily measured on all plotters by placing the cursor on the object. The distance is then read off the cursor data box (top left-hand corner in this case).

Use the side of a paper chart to measure distance with dividers

SPEED AND TIME

Having discovered how far it is from where you are to where you want to go, you'll probably want to know how long the trip will take, and how much fuel you may use. Because marine fuel consumption is generally measured in gallons per hour, rather than miles per gallon, you'll have to compare distance with time and speed as well. Speed at sea is measured in knots, which are nautical miles per hour (1 knot = 1.15 mph).

The relationship between distance, speed and time can be remembered by:
$$\text{Speed (S)} = \frac{\text{Distance (D) miles}}{\text{Time (T) hour}} \quad \text{or} \quad S = \frac{60 \times D \text{ (miles)}}{T \text{ (minutes)}}$$
Note that in the second equation, 60 converts hours to minutes

Calculating Speed. If you motored a distance of 2 nautical miles in 15 minutes, your speed would be calculated as 20 knots.
$$S = \frac{60 \times D}{T} = \frac{60 \times 2 \text{ nautical miles}}{15 \text{ minutes}} \qquad S = 8 \text{ knots}$$

Calculating Distance. If you have been motoring at 5 knots for 12 minutes, then you have run a distance of 2 miles.
$$D = \frac{S \times T}{60} = \frac{5 \text{ knots} \times 12 \text{ minutes}}{60} \qquad D = 1 \text{ miles}$$

Calculating Time. A distance of 10 miles is to be run at 6 knots. How long will the passage take?
$$T = \frac{D}{S} = \frac{10}{6} = \frac{5}{3} \qquad T = 1\ 2/3 \text{ hours or 1 hour and 40 minutes}$$

Realities of Speed. You can see your speed at a glance on most boats either by the speedometer or log (if you have one) or checking the SOG (Speed Over Ground) on the GPS. It is important to understand that the speedometer is reading the speed of the vessel through the water, while the GPS reads speed across the surface of the planet. If a current is running, GPS will include this in its SOG readout. Thus: 20 knots indicated on the speedometer when motoring into an adverse current of 2 knots leads to a SOG value of 18 knots. The same speed in a favoring current would read out as 22 knots SOG.

DIRECTION

Almost all paper charts are oriented with North at the top ("North-up"). If you start at North and turn right round to North again, you'll swivel through 360 degrees. All direction at sea is defined in terms of these degrees by using a compass.

Which Course is Real? Unlike a car, which is traveling in one direction at a given time, a boat's movement offers three choices. All are correct, but the difference is important:
• Heading is the direction the boat is pointing.
• Course Over Ground (COG or Track) is the direction the boat is traveling in across the surface of the planet. In a crosscurrent, this may well be different from the boat's heading. Most plotters can show you either, or both. Choose, and know which you have chosen. If in doubt, go for COG.
• Course desired is the course you need to make good to get to where you are going.

PART 6

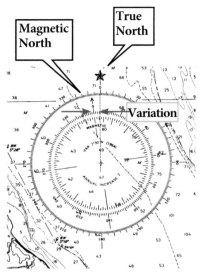

Variation can be either East or West. This example shows Magnetic North to the West of True North and is a West variation. The note inside the circles indicates a variation of 7° 30" W (West).

Compass Tips
- If a GPS gives your heading in degrees True, you will have to convert it to a magnetic heading for your compass by adding or subtracting the variation. Add for a West (W) variation and subtract for an East (E) variation.
- Know the position of the steering wheel for a straight course.
- Don't chase the compass.
- Motion can jostle a compass. Read it when the boat is steady.
- Don't stare at the compass. Have a reference to steer to, such as a buoy, a point of land, or a distant cloud.
- Remember the boat turns around the compass – the compass doesn't turn in the boat.

Compass Variation. Your boat's magnetic compass points to Magnetic North, but your charts are oriented to True North. The difference in degrees between your compass readings and True North is called variation. The amount and direction of variation will change depending on your location. The compass rose on your chart will indicate the amount and direction of the variation for your area.

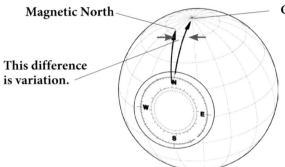

Magnetic North is not a fixed point like True North, but slowly wanders. The amount that it changes each year is also indicated on the compass rose as an annual increase or decrease.

Compass Deviation. Your compass responds to iron or steel objects which have magnetic properties. The difference in compass readings created by their magnetic influence is called the deviation. For instance, a bag of tools accidentally placed next to the compass can cause a deviation so that the compass reads 075 degrees when it should read 080 degrees. Even metal eyeglass frames may do it with a hand bearing compass.

Compass Variation on a GPS. A GPS often tells you the direction to or from something. It can do this in degrees True or degrees Magnetic. It's critical to know which it is, because in some places the discrepancy can be 20 degrees or more. A menu in most GPS sets and plotters allows the user to set the instrument to readout True or Magnetic. Either is fine, but you MUST know which it is.

THE WAYPOINT
A waypoint is a position of tactical interest chosen by the navigator. GPS will instantly give an activated waypoint's distance and bearing relative to the boat.

Inputting a Waypoint on a Plotter. To enter a waypoint using the plotter, open the waypoint menu, then move the cursor over the desired position on the chart for the waypoint and click on it. The plotter will automatically display the latitude and longitude numbers for the waypoint. This method avoids the potential human error problem of manually entering the lat/long numbers.

Inputting a Waypoint on a GPS from a Paper Chart. Use the chart to select the position of your desired waypoint, then determine its latitude and longitude using the method described earlier in "Plotting a Position on a Paper Chart" and input these numbers into the GPS. Once activated by pressing the GoTo button, the readout gives distance and bearing to the waypoint.

JUST HOW GOOD IS GPS

At its best, GPS is far more accurate than any ordinary boater needs. However, before risking one's boat, one or two caveats must be considered.

Chart Accuracy. In many countries charts are drawn with the utmost care, generally from meticulous survey data, but there are some areas in the world where this may not be the case. While GPS at sea can deliver a position good to 49 feet or less, the lines on a chart may be thicker than that, or the survey may have been conducted before GPS with a lesser degree of assumed accuracy. An electronic chart can often be zoomed in well beyond the intentions of the surveyor. Some plotters indicate when they're over-zoomed – perhaps with dots on the chart. Many do not. The answer is always to leave a seamanlike margin for reasonable error, and give rocks a wide berth.

Satellite Coverage. Once a GPS receiver is well "warmed up," satellite coverage is rarely an issue, but the instrument is only as good as the data its antenna is receiving. Check the satellite screen before you leave your slip, and take a look every so often to make sure all is well.

Datum. In the U.S. and many other areas of the world, GPS delivers its position using a lat/long datum called WGS84 (World Geodetic System 1984). However, a GPS may produce a position which is not consistent with the paper chart in use because the chart has been drawn to an older or different datum. It is possible to check a chart's datum in the title notes, then enter the GPS menus and make sure the one selected coincides. If the GPS or the plotter doesn't seem to coincide perfectly with reality, look for the buoys, use the depth sounder, and plenty of common sense.

Boat's position

Waypoint

This GPS satellite screen indicates signals are being received from 9 satellites and the accuracy of the GPS position is estimated as 10.6 feet. Four satellites are needed for a 3D fix (position and altitude). The position and number of satellites will vary as the earth rotates and the satellites change their positions in orbit. Satellite signals cannot penetrate solid objects. If used below deck in a boat, an external antenna may be needed.

PART 6

Here's a buoy on a chart plotter. For more details, place the cursor over it and press ENTER.

A box pops up with more information.

The Conventional Direction for lateral marks is a clockwise rotation around the U.S.

Caution
It is illegal to tie onto an aid to navigation or be in a position that prevents other vessels from seeing it.

AIDS TO NAVIGATION

Navigation aids are nautical road signs that can be used to help you determine your position, follow a safe course and to warn of dangers. Aids to navigation may be divided into two broad categories:

Buoys are floating marks anchored (moored) in a fixed position. Buoy positions depicted on a nautical chart are approximate within the swing movement allowed by the scope of their mooring cable. Be aware they can sometimes drag from their position as a result of storms, ice or impact with a ship.

Beacons are fixed to the sea bottom or located on shore, making them a reliable and precise aid for navigating. Beacons include daybeacons with a daymark, beacons with a light (lights), lighthouses, and ranges. Buoys and beacons with lights can be identified by their color (red, green, white, or yellow) and rhythm (pattern of their flashes). There are a variety of rhythms displayed by various lights. Most unlit marks have reflective tape that will be picked up by your searchlight. All marks are identified on charts. Anything floating (typically a buoy) is shown at an angle from the vertical, while fixed objects are straight up and down. NOTE: This is not necessarily the case with plotter charts.

There are four different navigation marking systems used in U.S. waters:
1 The U.S. Marking System is used on all navigable waters in the U.S., with the exception of the Mississippi River and its tributaries and the Intracoastal Waterway.
2 The Information and Regulatory Markers used on navigable state waters and non-navigable internal state waters.
3 The Intracoastal Waterway System used on the Intracoastal Waterway from New Jersey through Texas.
4 The Western River System used on the Mississippi River and its tributaries.

U.S. Marking System
Lateral Marks. A system of lateral marks is used to indicate on which side a mark should be passed when returning from seaward. In U.S. waters, red marks are kept on your right (starboard) side and green ones on your left (port) side. Remember this orientation by the "3 Rs" of "RED, RIGHT, RETURNING (from seaward)." When an approach from seaward cannot be determined, the Conventional Direction is used, which is a clockwise rotation around the U.S. land mass and northerly and westerly in the Great Lakes, except for southerly in Lake Michigan.

Preferred Channel Marks. When channels divide, one will be "preferred" for deeper draft vessels or as part of a continuing waterway. It may or may not be the one you want, but at the division you will find a preferred Light: same color as uppermost band (if lighted) and is a group flashing light, e.g., Gp Fl (2+1) 6s (2 flashes and 1 flash every 6 seconds) channel buoy. This may be passed on either side but will exhibit a preferred side based on the color of the uppermost band. If the main channel is to your left, when returning from seaward, the top band will be red indicating the buoy is to be passed on your right (starboard) side. If the top band is green that indicates the preferred channel is to the right and the buoy is to be passed on your left (port) side.
Color: red and green horizontal bands
Shape: cans, squares, nuns, and triangles
Character: letter (s)
Light: same color as uppermost band (if lighted) and is a group flashing light, e.g., Gp Fl (2+1) 6s (2 flashes and 1 flash every 6 seconds).

COMING INTO A HARBOR FROM OPEN WATER

Port (Left) Lateral Marks
Color: green
Shape: cans or squares
Character: odd numbers
Light: green (if lighted)

Starboard (Right) Lateral Marks
Color: red
Shape: nuns or triangles
Character: even numbers
Light: red (if lighted)

Cans have flat tops and odd numbers.

Nuns have pointed tops and even numbers.

A beacon with a square daymark and odd number marks the left side of a channel.

Can

Nun

Buoy with a light

Light and sound signals

A beacon with a triangle daymark and even number marks the right side of a channel.

Red buoys have an "R" indicating their color, while some greens may not have a "G". Note the odd number (G "3") on the green can and the even number (R "4") on the red nun. If a red or green buoy has a light and/or sound signal, this is indicated (Fl R 2.5s BELL).

These illustrations show a variety of safe water marks.

Safe Water Marks. These marks denote navigable (safe) water on all sides. They are frequently used to identify the middle of a channel or an offshore approach point to a channel.
Color: red and white vertical stripes
Shape: sphere or buoy with a red spherical topmark
Character: letter (s)
Light: white (if lighted) and flashes the Morse code (Mo) signal for the letter "A" (i.e., 1 short flash followed by 1 long flash). This lighted safe water buoy at the seaward approach to the Winyah Bay channel is identified by the symbols RW (red and white stripes) and Mo A (light flashes Morse code "A"). "WB" indicates it is the safe water mark for the Winyah Bay entrance.

Perferred Channel Bouys. This preferred channel buoy with a light is identified on the chart by RG "MH" Fl (2+1) R 6s. The RG symbol indicates that the top band is red (R), which tells us that the preferred channel is to the left. We can also identify the buoy by the letters "MH" on it.

Green top band indicates the preferred channel should be passed on your port side to take the preferred channel.

Isolated Danger Marks. These are placed near an isolated danger with navigable water all around. They have black and red horizontal bands with a topmark of two black spheres. If lighted, they display a group flashing of two white flashes every 5 seconds.

Special Purpose Marks. These are not navigation marks, but are used to alert you to a special feature or area such as the Triton submarine turning basin at the mouth of the St. Mary's River. They also mark pipelines, traffic separation schemes, spoil areas, and jetties. These marks can be identified by their yellow color with black letter(s). If lighted, they display a yellow fixed or flashing light. You will have to refer to a chart, Notices to Mariners, Coast Pilot or Light List to determine their meaning.

Information and Regulatory Markers These are used to alert you to dangers, exclusion and controlled areas, directions, and other regulatory matters and information. They have orange square, diamond or circle symbols with an orange band above and below the symbol displayed against a white background.

Special Purpose Mark

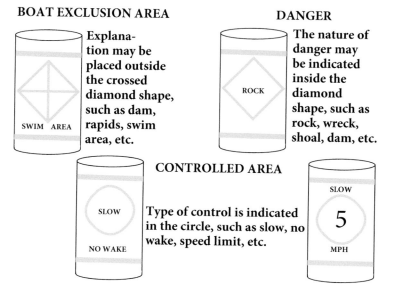

BOAT EXCLUSION AREA

SWIM AREA

Explanation may be placed outside the crossed diamond shape, such as dam, rapids, swim area, etc.

DANGER

ROCK

The nature of danger may be indicated inside the diamond shape, such as rock, wreck, shoal, dam, etc.

CONTROLLED AREA

SLOW

NO WAKE

Type of control is indicated in the circle, such as slow, no wake, speed limit, etc.

SLOW

5

MPH

INTRACOASTAL WATERWAY SYSTEM (ICW)

This waterway on the East Coast and the Gulf of Mexico uses its own unique markings of a yellow triangle **G** and a yellow square **L**. Since there is no obvious approach from seaward for the ICW, the Conventional Direction of clockwise rotation around the U.S. land mass is used. As a result, the marks toward the mainland side of the waterway are designated as marking the right side of the waterway by a yellow triangle **G**, and the ones toward the sea are the left side and marked with a yellow square **L**. When following the ICW from New Jersey to Texas, a yellow **G** should be left on the boat's starboard side and a yellow **L** on its port side, regardless of the color of the navigation aid on which they appear. The prudent navigator will follow charts closely and carry an up-to-date ICW cruising guide.

There are places along the Intracoastal Waterway where its waterway and a channel leading in from the sea coincide. If the directions of the two systems are the same, the yellow triangles will be on the red marks and the yellow squares on the green marks. But if the conventional direction of the ICW runs opposite to the "returning from seaward" direction of the channel, the U.S. Marking system for the channel prevails and the yellow triangles will be on the channel's green marks and the yellow squares on the red marks. Extreme care should be taken when passing the junction of the ICW and a channel leading in from the sea. The mixture of marks can be very confusing, but if you follow the yellow ICW symbols, you should not get lost.

Intracoastal Waterway

New Jersey

Texas

The Intracoastal Waterway is a network of protected inland water routes winding from New Jersey to Texas.

The yellow triangle on this red daymark indicates the starboard (mainland) side of the ICW channel.

The yellow square on this green daymark marks the port (seaward) side of the ICW channel.

ON-DECK SAFETY

Safety starts with prevention. Checking the boat for potential trouble spots and regularly inspecting equipment will go a long way towards ensuring a safe cruise. If things do start to go wrong, don't panic. Just assess the situation and remember: Keep control of the boat.

Make sure the sharp ends of cotter pins are turned back and taped to prevent injury.

When wires fray, they create **"meathooks"** or **"fishhooks"** which can cut your hands or tear the sails. Check your halyards and lifelines frequently.

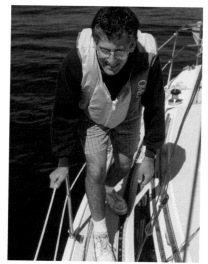

When moving around on deck remember..."One hand for the boat, and one hand for yourself."

Sloppy lines at the base of the mast can become jammed if you have to lower sails in an emergency.

STAYING ONBOARD

- Wear footwear with good wet traction.

- When moving forward to the mast or foredeck, it is safer to do so on the windward side of the boat.

- Lifelines work best if you keep your body low.

- Any openings in the rails of the bow and stern pulpit of lifelines should be securely closed while underway.

Don't put yourself in a danger zone. If the fairlead breaks (above), this crew member could be injured when the sheet snaps free.

OVERBOARD RESCUE

All sailors must know how to react quickly to a crew overboard situation. Losing sight of the PIW correlates very highly with loss of life. All of the following recovery methods involve four key elements:

1. Regaining contact.
2. Attaching PIW to the boat.
3. Getting PIW back aboard.
4. Giving after care.

Quick-Stop Rescue

The hallmark of the Quick-Stop rescue method is the immediate reduction of boat speed by turning to windward and thereafter maneuvering at modest speed, remaining near the person in water (PIW). Many consider this method superior to the conventional procedure of reaching off, then either jibing or tacking and returning on a reciprocal course, since the PIW is kept in sight throughout. The Quick-Stop requires a tack and a jibe; and jibing in heavy weather conditions may be difficult for some boats and crews. It is generally regarded as a good method for short-handed sailing. Here are the steps:

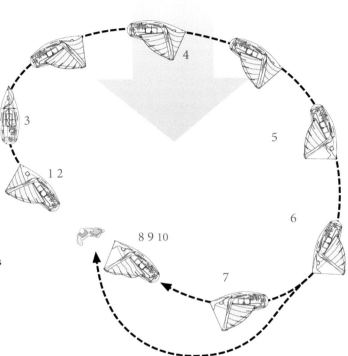

1 Shout "Crew Overboard!" and provide immediate flotation for the PIW. Throw buoyant objects such as cockpit cushions, life rings and so on as soon as possible. Even if these objects do not come to the aid of the PIW, they will "litter the water" where he or she went overboard and help your spotter to keep the PIW in view. Deployment of the overboard pole and flag (dan-buoy) requires too much time. The pole should be saved to "put on top" of the PIW in case the initial maneuver is unsuccessful.

2 Designate a crew member to spot and point to the PIW. The spotter should NEVER take his or her eyes off the PIW.

3 Bring the boat head-to-wind and beyond, leaving the headsail backed. If the overboard occurred off the wind, trim mainsail and headsail to close-hauled as the boat heads up. Keep turning with the headsail backed to further slow the boat until the wind is slightly abaft the beam. Do not release the sheets.

4 Head on a beam-to-broad reach course (approximately 90 to 120 degrees off the wind) for two or three boat lengths, then change course to nearly dead downwind.

5 Drop or furl the headsail (if possible) while keeping the mainsail centered (or nearly so). If the headsail is dropped, the headsail sheets should be kept tight to keep them and the sail inside the lifelines.

6 Jibe when the PIW is abeam or aft of abeam of the boat (timing of jibe depends on the boat's maneuverability and performance in existing wind and sea conditions).

7 Approach the PIW on a close reach course, adjusting speed with the mainsail; or glide up into the wind as you would when picking up a mooring. The approach will depend on your boat's maneuverability, position after your jibe, wind and sea conditions and helmsman's ability.

8 Stop the boat alongside the PIW and establish contact with a heaving line or other device. A rescue throw bag with 50 to 75 feet of light floating line can be thrown into the wind because the line is kept inside the bag and trails out as it sails to the PIW.

9 Attach the PIW to the boat.

10 Bring the PIW on board.

Figure-8 Rescue

For small inshore keelboats whose stability characteristics may result in loss of control during a jibe in heavy weather, the Quick-Turn (or Figure-8) rescue allows for a return to the PIW without jibing. Take the following steps in a Quick-Turn rescue:

1 As soon as a crew member falls overboard, throw buoyant objects, such as cushions, life jackets or life rings, to the PIW and shout "Crew overboard!"
2 Designate someone to spot and point at the person in the water. The spotter should NEVER take his or her eyes off the PIW.

3 Sail the boat on a beam reach for a maximum of four boat lengths.
4 Tack into the wind and fall off onto a very broad reach, crossing the boat's original course.
5 When downwind of the PIW, turn into the wind as if you were going to pick up a mooring.
6 Stop alongside the PIW by easing or backing sails.
7 Establish contact with the PIW with a heaving line or other device.
8 Recover the PIW on board.

Getting the PIW Aboard

Attaching the PIW to the boat. A weak link in overboard rescues is what happens after contact has been made. A PIW holding onto a line has been known to let it slip out of their grasp as they succumb to fatigue and hypothermia. Take immediate action to attach the PIW to the boat by clipping a line to the PIW harness or using a sling. Once attached to the boat, the PIW can be brought on board without fear of losing him or her. If rescue has been made with a Lifesling, properly clipped around the chest, this eliminates the problem.

Getting back aboard. Except in calm conditions, lifting a PIW aboard can be far from easy. It must be borne in mind that there will certainly be some degree of shock, an injury may have been sustained and hypothermia may be setting in.

Boarding by ladder. If the swim ladder is mounted over the stern, be careful lest the boat's pitching causes the ladder or hull to injure the PIW. Consider other means if this possibility seems real. In the case of a simple trip over the rails on a calm afternoon, however, the stern ladder is your first and obvious way.

Lifting by sling. The over-riding advantage of the Lifesling is that the PIW can be lifted on to the boat. This involves hoisting the person using a halyard. A block and tackle can be used as well. Practice using the sling, as an emergency is not the first time to try this.

Aftercare. Take the greatest care of the PIW who often succumb to hypothermia (see page 99, "Hypothermia").

Under Power Rescue

There may be occasions when a quick rescue under sail is not possible. For instance, if you're motoring along under power or there is not enough wind, or in the worst case scenario, the mast has failed and gone overboard, take the following steps:

1 As soon as a crew member falls overboard, throw buoyant objects, such as cushions, life jackets or life rings, to the PIW and shout "Crew overboard!"
2 Designate someone to spot and point at the PIW. The spotter should NEVER take his or her eyes off the PIW.
3 Return to the PIW. Make sure all sheets and lines are on board the boat and secured before turning on the engine and putting it into gear. While making the rescue, maintain constant vigilance that no lines go overboard.
4 Approach the PIW with the boat headed into the wind and under very slow speed. Stop the boat alongside the PIW.
5 Establish contact with the PIW with a heaving line or other device, and stop the engine.
6 Bring the PIW on board. Make sure the PIW does not get near the propeller at any time during the recovery procedure.

Lifesling-Type Rescue

If there are few people on board, the Lifesling-type rescue method should be employed. The Lifesling is a floating harness that is deployed from the boat's stern with a long floating line attached. The end of the line is attached to the boat. Once the PIW reaches the harness, he or she places the sling around his or her body, and is attached to the boat from that point on until being lifted out of the water. The success of this method depends on the PIW grabbing the line and putting on the sling. It takes longer than the Quick-Stop and the other methods, but provides a means for a single crew member to effect a rescue of a PIW.

1 As soon as a crew member falls overboard, throw a cushion or other buoyant objects to the PIW and shout "Crew Overboard!" while the boat is brought IMMEDIATELY head-to-wind, slowed and stopped. The main is trimmed to centerline.

2 The Lifesling is deployed by opening the bag that is hung on the stern pulpit and dropping the sling into the water. It will trail out astern and draw out the remaining line.

3 Once the Lifesling is deployed, the boat is sailed in a wide circle around the PIW with the line and sling trailing astern. The jib is not tended but allowed to back from the head-to-wind position, which increases the rate of turn.

4 Contact is established with the PIW by the line and sling being drawn inward by the boat's circling motion. The PIW then places the sling over his or her head and under his or her arms.

5 Upon contact, the boat is put head-to-wind again, the headsail is dropped to the deck or furled and the mainsail is doused.

6 As the boat drifts, the crew begins pulling the sling and the PIW to the boat. If necessary a cockpit winch can be used to assist in this phase, which should continue until the PIW is alongside and pulled up tightly until he or she is suspended in the sling (so that the PIW will not drop out and the torso is out of the water).

This system is effective if the line length is preadjusted to avoid running over the line, and if the method is practiced to achieve competence.

The Lifesling is a floating device attached to the boat by a length of floating line that doubles as a hoisting sling to retrieve a PIW in the water. If the side of the boat is too high to reach the PIW, or the PIW is injured, the sling can be used to hoist the person up and over the lifelines.

PART 7

RUNNING AGROUND

It's hard to find sailors who haven't stuck their keel into the mud at least once. Usually, the only damage is a bruised ego, but running aground can be serious if you slam into a rock. You can often get yourself free and sailing again if you know what to do. First, check the bilge of the boat to make sure the impact hasn't caused any leaking. Figure out if you can simply wait for the incoming tide to lift you off the bottom. You have to be more aggressive in freeing yourself by backing off, kedging, or heeling.

Backing Off Under Power
By putting the engine in reverse and keeping the rudder straight, you may be able to back yourself off the shoal.

Kedging
Using your anchor, you can also pull yourself free (kedge off). Use your dinghy to carry the anchor directly astern until you reach a scope of about 5:1. Lead the anchor line to a cockpit sheet winch and grind the line in with the rudder straight.

Heeling Boat
You can decrease the boat's draft by heeling over. Swing the boom out to the side and have members of the crew sit on it. This may free the keel from the bottom. The main halyard should be used at the end of the boom to reinforce the topping lift. Remember, heeling a winged keel boat may only dig the wing in deeper.

HYPOTHERMIA, SEASICKNESS AND HEAT EMERGENCIES

Sailing can expose you to extreme conditions, both hot and cold. On hot windless days, you'll be exposed to a lot of sun. On windy, overcast days, the cool spray coming over the bow can send a chill down your spine. Be prepared for these changes. Drink lots of water and wear clothing that protects your skin and head from the sun. Have warm clothing along in case the weather turns foul. Put on your jacket or pants before you get cold. In addition, you should know the warning signals for heat and cold emergencies and what to do in those situations.

HEAT EXHAUSTION

SIGNALS...
- Cool, moist, pale skin
- Heavy sweating
- Headache
- Dizziness
- Nausea
- Weakness, exhaustion

TREATMENT...
Without prompt care, heat exhaustion can advance to a more serious condition — heat stroke. First aid includes:
- Move person to cool environment.
- Remove clothing soaked with perspiration and loosen any tight clothing.
- Apply cool, wet towels or sheets.
- Fan the person.
- Give person a half glass (4 oz.) of cool water every 15 minutes.

HEAT STROKE

SIGNALS...
- Red, hot, dry or moist skin
- Very high temperature
- Changes in level of consciousness
- Vomiting
- Rapid, weak pulse
- Rapid, shallow breathing

TREATMENT...
Heat stroke is life threatening. Anyone suffering from heat stroke needs to be cooled and an EMS technician should be contacted immediately. To care for heat stroke:
- Move person to cool environment.
- Apply cool, wet towels or sheets.
- If available, place ice or cold packs on the person's wrists and ankles, groin, each armpit, and neck.
- If unconscious, check breathing and pulse.

SEASICKNESS

You can reduce your chances of becoming seasick by getting plenty of sleep the night before you go sailing.
- Eat before going out, but avoid greasy, heavy foods and alcohol.
- Dress warmly.
- Some people use wrist bands that activate accupressure points. Others rely on prescription medications such as Scopolamine.
- Symptoms include yawning, burping, paleness, a headache or nausea . Get on deck for fresh air and watch the horizon to calm your sensory system. Better yet, steer the boat. Eating salted crackers or drinking a carbonated cola drink might help. In really bad cases, lie on your back in a spot where you're sheltered from cold and spray.

HYPOTHERMIA

SIGNALS...
- Shivering
- Impaired judgment
- Dizziness
- Numbness
- Change in level of consciousness
- Weakness
- Glassy stare
  (Physical symptoms may vary, since age, body size, and clothing will cause individual differences.)

TREATMENT...
Medical assistance should be given to anyone with hypothermia. Until medical assistance arrives, these steps should be taken:
- Check breathing and pulse.
- Move the person to a warm place.
- Remove all wet clothing. Gradually warm the person by wrapping in blankets or putting on dry clothes. Do not warm a person too quickly, such as immersing in warm water. Rapid rewarming may cause dangerous heart rhythms. Hot water bottles and chemical heat packs may be used if first wrapped in a towel or blanket before applying.
- Give warm, nonalcoholic and non-caffeinated liquids to a conscious person only.

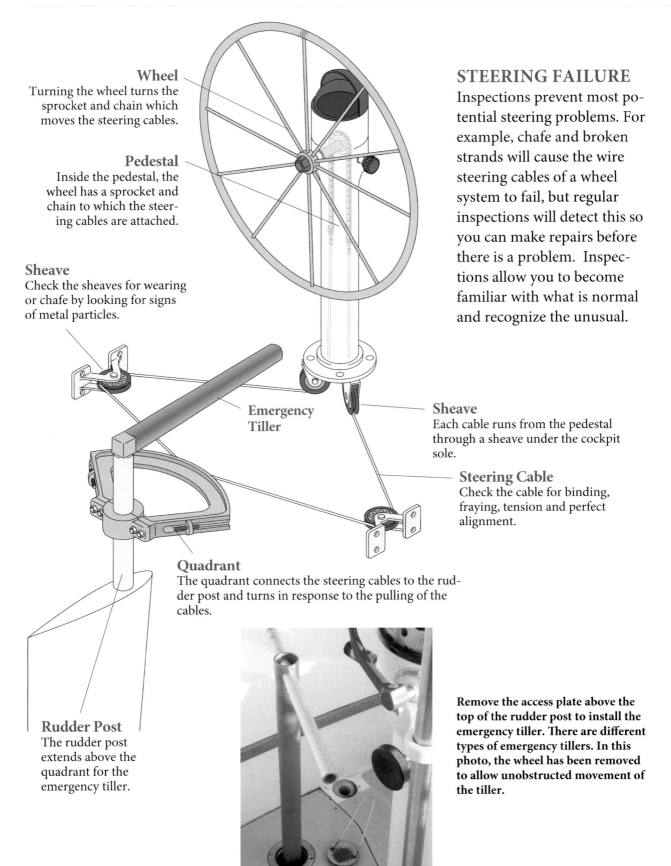

Wheel
Turning the wheel turns the sprocket and chain which moves the steering cables.

Pedestal
Inside the pedestal, the wheel has a sprocket and chain to which the steering cables are attached.

Sheave
Check the sheaves for wearing or chafe by looking for signs of metal particles.

Emergency Tiller

Quadrant
The quadrant connects the steering cables to the rudder post and turns in response to the pulling of the cables.

Rudder Post
The rudder post extends above the quadrant for the emergency tiller.

STEERING FAILURE
Inspections prevent most potential steering problems. For example, chafe and broken strands will cause the wire steering cables of a wheel system to fail, but regular inspections will detect this so you can make repairs before there is a problem. Inspections allow you to become familiar with what is normal and recognize the unusual.

Sheave
Each cable runs from the pedestal through a sheave under the cockpit sole.

Steering Cable
Check the cable for binding, fraying, tension and perfect alignment.

Remove the access plate above the top of the rudder post to install the emergency tiller. There are different types of emergency tillers. In this photo, the wheel has been removed to allow unobstructed movement of the tiller.

FIRE SAFETY

Most fires on cruising boats can be traced to fuel leaks or electrical failures. Regulations require sailboats to carry up-to-date fire extinguishers, and for your safety, be sure you know where they are located and how to operate them.

Combustion occurs when three ingredients are present.

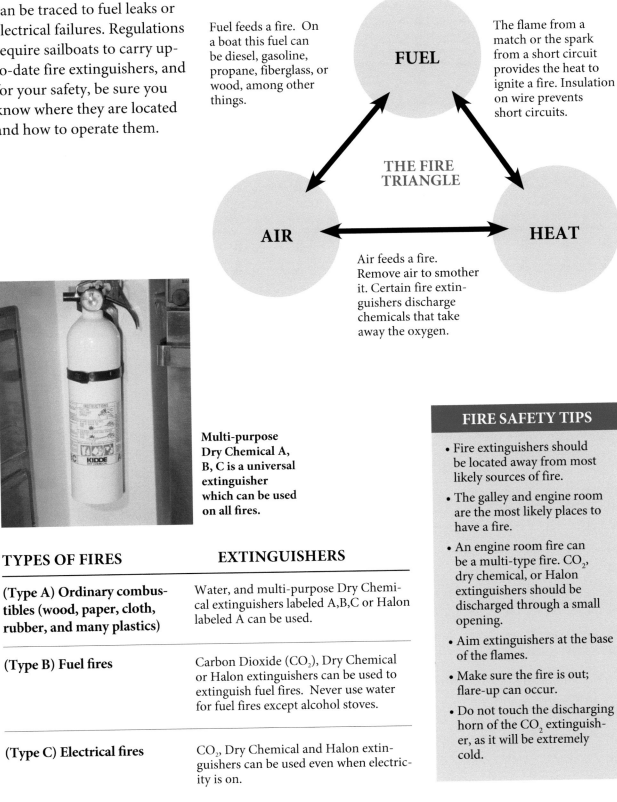

Fuel feeds a fire. On a boat this fuel can be diesel, gasoline, propane, fiberglass, or wood, among other things.

FUEL

The flame from a match or the spark from a short circuit provides the heat to ignite a fire. Insulation on wire prevents short circuits.

THE FIRE TRIANGLE

AIR

HEAT

Air feeds a fire. Remove air to smother it. Certain fire extinguishers discharge chemicals that take away the oxygen.

Multi-purpose Dry Chemical A, B, C is a universal extinguisher which can be used on all fires.

FIRE SAFETY TIPS

- Fire extinguishers should be located away from most likely sources of fire.
- The galley and engine room are the most likely places to have a fire.
- An engine room fire can be a multi-type fire. CO_2, dry chemical, or Halon extinguishers should be discharged through a small opening.
- Aim extinguishers at the base of the flames.
- Make sure the fire is out; flare-up can occur.
- Do not touch the discharging horn of the CO_2 extinguisher, as it will be extremely cold.

TYPES OF FIRES	EXTINGUISHERS
(Type A) Ordinary combustibles (wood, paper, cloth, rubber, and many plastics)	Water, and multi-purpose Dry Chemical extinguishers labeled A,B,C or Halon labeled A can be used.
(Type B) Fuel fires	Carbon Dioxide (CO_2), Dry Chemical or Halon extinguishers can be used to extinguish fuel fires. Never use water for fuel fires except alcohol stoves.
(Type C) Electrical fires	CO_2, Dry Chemical and Halon extinguishers can be used even when electricity is on.

TOWING

In some emergencies, such as being hard aground or suffering engine failure, you may have to request or accept a tow from another boat. Use a strong line like your anchor rode and attach it to a strong part of your boat. Start the tow slowly. Increase the length of the towing line as you increase speed.

Towing Bridle
Tie a bowline in the end of the towing line at the foredeck and lead another strong line through it, anchoring each end on the jib winches in the cockpit.

Bow Bridle
Divide the load on the towline by leading a bridle from the end of the towline to two cleats on the foredeck. Make sure the cleats are through-bolted to substantial backing plates in order to carry the load.

FLOODING

A broken port or hatch or a hole in the hull can flood your boat. Your bilge pump will help remove the water, and you may have to use buckets to bail by hand if the situation becomes serious. Cover a port or a hatch by screwing, nailing or tying on pieces of wood, which can sometimes be found under your mattresses or the cabin sole. For holes in the hull, tie a mattress or a sail over the puncture on the outside. Use cushions, sail bags or clothing to plug the opening from the inside.

- If possible, heel the boat over so that the hole stays above water.
- Make sure the water in the bilge contains no small debris, such as wood, fiberglass, paint or dirt, that will clog the pump's intake.
- If you're in danger of sinking, make sure everyone on board is wearing a life jacket and knows the procedure for abandoning ship, including how to make an emergency broadcast on VHF.

Flares can be hand-held or shot into the air with a special gun to signal distress.

You can also call for help by repeatedly blasting an air horn to attract attention.

SIGNALING FOR HELP

Before you decide to ask for outside assistance, determine if you can take care of the problem yourself. You may be able to get back to the harbor under your own power, or accept a tow from a friendly boat. U.S. Coast Guard and private search-and-rescue missions are expensive and time-consuming. If you do need to signal for help, use the signals, either separately or together, that are recognized by the U.S. Coast Guard and the Navigation Rules.

International Distress Signals
- A smoke signal giving off orange-colored smoke.
- A rocket parachute flare or a hand flare showing a red light.
- Rockets or shells, throwing red stars fired one at a time at short intervals.
- Continuous sounding of a foghorn.
- "Mayday" spoken over a radiotelephone.
- A signal consisting of a square flag having above or below it a ball or anything resembling a ball.
- Slowly and repeatedly waving both outstretched arms.
- A radiotelegraph or radiotelephone alarm signal.
- Signals transmitted by an emergency position-indicating radio beacon (EPIRB).

SAFETY EQUIPMENT

The U.S. Coast Guard requires sailboats to carry certain safety equipment. If you're not sure that you have all the items you need to meet the official requirements, you can obtain the pamphlet entitled "Federal Requirements for Recreational Boats" from your local chandlery, U.S. Coast Guard stations or by searching the website (www.uscg.mil). Listed here is a summary of the minimum required safety gear, which should be supplemented by the boat owner. Also, local governments may have their own safety requirements to which you should comply.

- U.S. Coast Guard approved life jackets, of Type I, II, III, or V are required for each person aboard the vessel. At least one Type IV (throwable) must also be on board. The life jackets need to be readily accessible and of the appropriate size for passengers on the boat. The Type IV life jacket must be immediately available while underway.
- Boats less than 39 feet must carry a whistle or horn or some other efficient sound producing device. All boats 39 feet and longer must have a whistle or horn with a range of at least 1/2 mile or more (for larger vessels), as well as a bell.
- U.S. Coast Guard approved Visual Distress Signals must be carried by all boats except those that are: less than 16 feet in length, participating in organized events such as regattas, open sailboats less than 26 feet in length without auxiliary power, or manually propelled boats. Don't display any of these signals unless you need emergency assistance.

- U.S. Coast Guard approved fire extinguishers must be carried aboard all auxiliary powered vessels.
- Boats less than 26 feet long must have one Type B-1. Boats 26 to 40 feet long must have two Type B-1s or one Type B-2.
- Navigation lights must be displayed between sunset and sunrise while underway or anchored.
- A boat sailing and being propelled by an engine at the same time (motorsailing) must display, where it can best be seen, an inverted conical shape. (Boats less than 12 meters long are exempted from this requirement).
- Boats with inboard gasoline engines must have flame arrestors. Most boats with auxiliary engines must also be ventilated.
- During the day, sailboats at anchor shall exhibit forward, where best seen, a ball shape.
- Vessels restricted in their ability to maneuver because of diving operations or activity must display a rigid replica of the code flag "A".

Recommended Safety Gear
- Additional means of propulsion, including oars, paddles or an outboard motor.
- Manual bailing devices, such as buckets or bilge pumps.
- A basic first aid kit with instructions.
- An anchor and anchor line.
- A radar reflector.
- A tool kit, spare parts and through-hull plugs.
- A portable VHF radio.
- Navigation charts and compass.
- Lifesling, a flotation device with attached line for retrieving crew from the water. Especially useful when sailing with just one or two crew.

A radar reflector hung in the boat's rigging will alert other vessels of your presence in periods of restricted visibility.

Permanently mounted radar reflector

Hoisted radar reflector

FEDERAL SAFETY REQUIREMENTS

The U.S. Coast Guard is the federal law enforcement agency for boating. When you are sailing and are hailed by a Coast Guard vessel, you are required to heave-to or drop sails so that an inspection officer may board. Other local, state or federal law enforcement agencies may also board and examine your boat.

Each U.S. Coast Guard vessel has a distinctive stripe on the hull and the words "U.S. Coast Guard" on the side of the vessel. There are uniformed, armed U.S. Coast Guard personnel aboard each vessel.

Boarding Inspection

A U.S. Coast Guard boarding officer finding a boat operating in an unsafe condition may require it to return to port immediately. Conditions that may cause termination of use are:
- Insufficient U.S. Coast Guard approved life jackets.
- Insufficient fire extinguishers.
- Overloaded conditions, i.e. exceeds listing on the capacity plate or obviously inadequate for the number of people on board.
- Improper navigation light display.
- Fuel leakage.
- Fuel in bilges.
- Improper ventilation.
- Improper backfire flame control.
- Manifestly unsafe voyage, i.e. unsafe vessel, weather conditions, or hazardous situation which could result in injury or death, or require rescue.

Additional Basic Regulations

- Operating a boat under the influence of drugs or alcohol may result in a civil penalty or a criminal action.
- Negligent or Grossly Negligent Operation of a vessel which endangers lives and property is prohibited by law.
- Improper use of a radiotelephone (VHF) is a criminal offense.
- Boating accidents should be reported to the nearest state authority per the federal requirement.
- You are obligated to render as much assistance as can be safely provided to anyone in danger at sea.

The Float Plan

Before you leave for a day of sailing, it is a good idea to tell someone else your plans. Leave a float plan with a friend or relative who can contact the U.S. Coast Guard or other agencies in the event you don't return on schedule. The following information should be included:

- Name and phone number of the person reporting: Peter James, 413-5234.
- Complete description of the boat including type, color, registration number, sail number or insignia, length, etc: sailboat, sloop rig, white hull, light blue deck, CF0067 LK, Sail #4546, 30-foot, "Snoopy."
- List of people on board including name, age, address & phone: Bob James, 38, Susie James, 35, Eric James, 10, all live at 436 Walnut St, Livermore, 446-2141.
- Method of communication (i.e. VHF radio, cellular phone, etc.).
- Survival gear aboard: 4 life jackets, 1 Lifesling, 3 smoke flares.
- Trip Plan: Leaving at 0800 from Marina Village, Pier 8 going to Angel Island. Expect to return by 1700 and in no event later than 2000.
- If not returned by 2200 call the U.S. Coast Guard or Police at 911.

APPENDIX

The **cutter** is a sloop with its mast near the middle of the hull, allowing space to fly a second jib.

The **yawl** has two masts. Its mizzen mast is behind the rudder post.

The **ketch** is another two masted boat. The mizzen mast is in front of the rudder post.

The **schooner** has two or more masts, with the tallest usually aft.

The marconi-rigged **sloop** is the most common modern rig. It's excellent for sailing upwind.

A cat rig has no jib. This two-masted example is also a ketch rig. Hence the name **cat ketch**.

Most modern **multihulls** are sloop-rigged. Their mainsails have full-length battens and a large curved roach.

The traditional **gaff rig** has a four-sided mainsail with a gaff attached to the top.

HULL TYPES

A monohull is a boat with a single hull.

The twin-hulled catamaran features speed and acceleration.

The three-hulled trimaran can also carry a lot of sail for speed.

The traditional **full keel** allows for a deep interior and excellent straight-line tracking.

The **fin keel and spade rudder** reduces drag and improves maneuverability.

A deep **"wineglass" hull** provides gentle motion and ample interior volume.

A shallow hull with a **fin keel** is a great performer, especially downwind.

A **winged-keel** allows a shallow keel to perform more efficiently.

A **bulb keel** concentrates weight at its bottom, improving stability.

Some small keelboats have retractable **outboard rudders** which allow them to travel in shallow waters and swing back on impact.

A **spade rudder** is efficient but unprotected from impact.

A **skeg-mounted rudder** is strong and well protected.

APPENDIX

GLOSSARY OF SAILING TERMS
Including the phonetic alphabetic terms for radio use (in parentheses)

A (Alpha)

Abeam - off the side of (at right angle to) the boat.

Aboard - on the boat.

Adrift - a boat drifting without control.

Aft - at or toward the stern or behind the boat.

Aground - a boat whose keel is touching the bottom.

Alternator - a device which generates electricity from an engine.

Amidships - toward the center of the boat.

Apparent wind - the wind aboard a moving boat.

Astern - behind the stern of the boat.

Athwartships - across the boat from side to side.

B (Bravo)

Backstay - the standing rigging running from the stern to the top of the mast, keeping the mast from falling forward.

Back - 1.- to stop or to propel a boat backward by holding the clew of a sail out to windward. 2.- a counterclockwise change of wind direction.

Bail - to empty a boat of water.

Ballast - weight in the keel of a boat that provides stability.

Barometer - a weather forecasting instrument that measures air pressure.

Batten - a thin slat that slides into a pocket in the leech of a sail, helping it hold its shape.

Battery switch - the main electrical cutoff switch.

Beam - the width of a boat at its widest point.

Beam reach - (point of sail) sailing in a direction at approximately 90 degrees to the wind.

Bear away - to fall off, head away from the wind.

Bearing - the direction from one object to another expressed in degrees.

Beating - a course sailed upwind.

Below - the area of a boat beneath the deck.

Bend - to attach a sail to a spar or a headstay, or to attach a line to a sail.

Berth - 1. - the area in which you park your boat; 2. - the area in which you sleep on a boat.

Bight - doubling a line back on itself.

Bilge - the lowest part of the boat's interior, where water on board will collect.

Bitter end - the end of a line.

Blanket - to use a sail or object to block the wind from filling a sail.

Block - a pulley on a boat.

Boat hook - a pole with a hook on the end used for grabing hold of a mooring or retrieving somthing that has fallen overboard.

Boat speed - the speed of a boat through the water.

Bolt rope - the rope sewn into the foot and luff of some mainsails and the luff of some jibs by which the sails are attached to the boat.

Boom - the spar extending directly aft from the mast to which the foot of the mainsail is attached.

Boom vang - a block and tackle system which pulls the boom down to assist sail control.

Bottom - 1. - the underside of the boat. 2. - the land under the water.

Bow - the forward part of the boat.

Bow line (BOW - line) - a line running from the bow of the boat to the dock or mooring.

Bowline - (BOE-lin) - a knot designed to make a loop that will not slip and can be easily untied.

Breast line - a short dockline leading off the beam of the boat directly to the dock.

Broach - an uncontrolled rounding up into the wind, usually from a downwind point of sail.

Broad reach - (point of sail) sailing in a direction with the wind over the rear corner of the boat.

Bulkhead - a wall that runs athwartships on a boat, usually providing structural support to the hull.

Bunk - see **berth**, definition #2

Buoy - a floating navigation marker.

Buoyancy - the ability of an object to float.

By the lee - sailing on a run with the wind coming over the same side of the boat as the boom.

C (Charlie)

Cabin - the interior of a boat.

Can - an odd-numbered, green buoy marking the left side of a channel as you return to port.

Capsize - to tip or turn a boat over.

Cast off - to release a line when leaving a dock or mooring.

Catamaran - a twin-hulled sailing vessel with a deck or trampoline between the hulls.

Catboat - a boat with only a mainsail and the mast located at the bow.

Centerline - the midline of a boat running from bow to stern.

Center of Effort - the focal point of the force of the wind on the sails.

Center of Lateral Resistance - the focal point of the force of the water on the underbody of the boat.

Chafe - wear on a line or wire caused by rubbing.

Chainplates - strong metal plates which connect the shrouds to the boat.

Channel - a (usually narrow) path in the water, marked by buoys, in which the water is deep enough to sail.

Chart - a nautical map.

Charter - to rent a boat.

Chock - a guide mounted on the deck through which docklines and anchor rode are run.

Choke - a device for controlling the mixture of air and fuel for an engine.

Chop - rough, short, steep waves.

Cleat - a nautical fitting that is used to secure a line.

Clew - the lower, aft corner of a sail. The clew of the mainsail is held taut by the outhaul. The jib sheets are attached to the clew of the jib.

Close-hauled - the point of sail that is closest to the wind.

Close reach - (point of sail) sailing in a direction with the wind forward of the beam.

Coaming - the short protective wall surrounding the cockpit.

Cockpit - the lower area in which the steering controls and sail controls are located.

Coil - to loop a line neatly so it can be stored.

Come about - see **tack**.

Companionway - the steps leading from the cockpit or deck to the cabin below.

Compass - the magnetic instrument which indicates the direction in which the boat is headed.

Compass protractor - a plotting instrument oriented to latitude-longitude lines.

Compass rose - the twin circles on a chart which indicate the direction of true north and magnetic north.

Course - the direction in which the boat is steered.

Crew - besides the skipper, anyone on board who helps sail the boat.

Cringle - a ring sewn into the sail through which a line can be passed.

Cunningham - a line running through a cringle about eight inches up from the tack of a mainsail that is used to tighten the luff of the sail.

Current - the horizontal movement of water caused by tides, wind and other forces.

Cutter - a single-masted boat with the mast near the middle that is capable of flying both a jib and a staysail.

D (Delta)

Daysailer - a small sailboat.

Dead downwind - sailing in a direction straight downwind.

Deck - the mostly flat surface area on top of the boat.

Deck plate - a covered opening on deck leading to the water or fuel tanks, used for pumping out the holding tank or for access to the rudder post in case you need to install the emergency tiller.

Depower - to release the power from the sails by allowing them to luff or making them flatter. This is done to reduce heel.

Dinghy - a small sailboat or rowboat.

Displacement - the weight of a boat; therefore the amount of water it displaces.

Divider - instrument used for measuring distances or coordinates on a chart.

Dock - 1. - the wooden structure where a boat may be tied up. 2. - the act of bringing the boat to rest alongside the structure.

Dockline - a line used to secure the boat to the dock.

Dodger - a canvas protection in front of the cockpit of some boats that is designed to keep spray off the skipper and crew.

Downhaul - a line used to pull down on the movable gooseneck on some boats to tighten the luff of the mainsail. The cunningham has the same function on other boats.

Downwind - away from the direction of the wind.

Draft - the depth of a boat's keel from the water's surface.

E (Echo)

Ease - to let out a line or sail.

Ebb - an outgoing tidal current.

EPIRB - Emergency Position-Indicating Radio Beacon

F (Foxtrot)

Fairlead - a fitting that guides a jib sheet or other lines back to the cockpit or along the deck.

Fairway - the center of a channel.

Fall off - see **head down**.

Fast - secured.

Fathom - a measurement of the depth of water. One fathom equals six feet.

Fender - a rubber bumper used to protect a boat by keeping it from hitting a dock.

Fend off - push off.

Fetch - a course on which a boat can make its destination without having to tack.

Fishhooks - frayed wire that can cut your skin or rip sails.

Fitting - a piece of nautical hardware.

Flake - to lay out a line on deck using large loops to keep it from becoming tangled.

Flood - an incoming tidal current.

Float plan - an itinerary of your intended sailing trip, left with a responsible party onshore.

Following sea - waves hitting the boat from astern.

Foot - the bottom edge of a sail.

Fore - forward.

Forepeak - a storage area in the bow (below the deck).

Foresail - a jib or a genoa.

Forestay - the standing rigging running from the bow to the mast to which the jib is hanked on.

Forward - toward the bow.

Fouled - tangled.

Foul-weather gear - water-resistant clothing.

Freeboard - the height of the hull above the water's surface.

Full - not luffing.

Furl - to fold or roll up a sail.

G (Golf)

Gaff - on some boats, a spar along the top edge of a four-sided sail.

Gear - generic term for sailing equipment.

Genoa - a large jib whose clew extends aft of the mast.

Give-way vessel - the vessel required to give way to another boat when they may be on a collision course.

Glide zone - the distance a sailboat takes to coast to a stop.

Gooseneck - the strong fitting that connects the boom to the mast.

Grommet - a reinforcing metal ring set in a sail.

Ground tackle - the anchor and rode (chain and line).

Gudgeon - a fitting attached to the stern of a boat into which the pintles of a rudder are inserted.

Gunwale (GUNN-nle) - the edge of the deck where it meets the topsides.

Gust - see **puff**.

H (Hotel)

Halyard - a line used to hoist or lower a sail.

Hank - a snap hook that is used to connect the luff of a jib onto the forestay.

"Hard a-lee" - the command given to the crew just prior to tacking.

Hard over - to turn the tiller or wheel as far as possible in one direction.

Hatch - a large covered opening in the deck.

Hatch boards - boards that close off the companionway.

Haul in - to tighten a line.

Head - 1. - the top corner of a sail. 2. - the bathroom on a boat. 3. - the toilet on a boat.

Headboard - the reinforcing board affixed to the head of a sail.

Header - a wind shift which makes your boat head down or sails to be sheeted in.

Heading - the direction of the boat expressed in compass degrees.

Head down - to fall off, changing course away from the wind.

Head off - see **head down**.

Head up - to come up, changing course toward the wind.

Headsail - a jib, genoa, or staysail.

Headstay - the standing rigging running from the bow to the top of the mast.

Head-to-wind - the course of the boat when the bow is dead into the wind.

Headway - progress made forward.

Heave - to throw.

Heave-to - to hold one's position in the water by using the force of the sails and rudder to counter one another.

Heavy weather - strong winds and large waves.

Heel - the lean of a boat caused by the wind.

Helm - the tiller or wheel.

Helmsman - the person responsible for steering the boat.

High side - the windward side of the boat.

Hike - to position crew members out over the windward rail to help balance the boat.

Hiking stick - see **tiller extension**.

Holding ground - the bottom ground in an anchorage used to hold the anchor.

Hove-to - a boat that has completed the process of heaving-to, with its jib aback, its main loosely trimmed, and its rudder securely positioned to steer it close to the wind.

Hull - the body of the boat, excluding rig and sails.

Hull speed - the theoretical maximum speed of a sailboat determined by the length of its waterline.

I (India)

Inboard - inside of the rail of a boat.

In irons - a boat that is head-to-wind, making no forward headway.

J (Juliet)

Jacklines - sturdy wire, rope or webbing securely fastened at its ends on deck which permits the crew to hook in with their safety harnesses.

Jib - the forward sail of a boat attached to the forestay.

Jibe - to change direction of a boat by steering the stern through the wind.

"Jibe-ho" - the command given to the crew when starting a jibe.

Jiffy reef - a quick reefing system allowing a section of the mainsail to be tied to the boom.

Jury rig - an improvised, temporary repair.

K (Kilo)

Kedge off - to use an anchor to pull a boat into deeper water after it has run aground.

Keel - the heavy vertical fin beneath a boat that helps keep it upright and prevents it from slipping sideways in the water.

Ketch - a two-masted boat with its mizzen (after) mast shorter than its mainmast and located forward of the rudder post.

King spoke - a marker on the steering wheel which indicates when the rudder is centered.

Knockdown - a boat heeled so far that one of its spreaders touches the water.

Knot - one nautical mile per hour.

L (Lima)

Land breeze - a wind that blows over land and out to sea.

Lash - to tie down.

Lay - to sail a course that will clear an obstacle without tacking.

Lazarette - a storage compartment built into the deck.

Lazy sheet - the windward side jib sheet that is not under strain.

Lead (LEED) - to pass a line through a fitting or a block.

Lee helm - the boat's tendency to turn away from the wind.

Lee shore - land which is on the leeward side of the boat. Because the wind is blowing in that direction, a lee shore could pose a danger.

Leech - the after edge of a sail.

Leech line - an adjustable cord sewn into the back edge of a sail to prevent fluttering

Leeward - (LEW-erd) - the direction away from the wind (where the wind is blowing to).

Leeward side - the side of the boat or sail that is away from the wind.

Leeway - sideways slippage of the boat in a direction away from the wind.

Lifeline - plastic coated wire, supported by stanchions, around the outside of the deck to help prevent crew members from falling overboard.

Lifesling - a floating device attached to the boat by a length of floating line that doubles as a hoisting sling to retrieve a PIW in the water.

Lift - 1. - the force that results from air passing by a sail, or water past a keel, that moves the boat forward and sideways. 2. - a change in wind direction which lets the boat head up.

Line - rope in use on a boat.

Line stoppers - levered cleats which hold lines under load and can be released easily.

Low side - the leeward side of the boat.

Lubber's line - a small post in a compass used to help determine a course or a bearing.

Luff - 1. - the forward edge of a sail.
2. - the fluttering of a sail caused by aiming too close to the wind.

Lull - a decrease in wind speed for a short duration.

M (Mike)

Magnetic - in reference to magnetic north rather than true north.

Mainmast - the taller of two masts on a boat.

Mainsail (MAIN-sil) - the sail hoisted on the mast of a sloop or cutter or the sail hoisted on the mainmast of a ketch or yawl.

Mainsheet - the controlling line for the mainsail.

Marlinspike - a pointed tool used to loosen knots.

Mast - the large aluminum or wooden pole in the middle of a boat from which the mainsail is set.

Master switch - see **battery switch**.

Masthead - the top of the mast.

Masthead fly - a wind direction indicator on top of the mast.

Mast step - the structure that the bottom of the mast sits on.

Mayday - the internationally recognized distress signal for a life-threatening emergency.

Mizzen - the small aftermost sail on a ketch or yawl hoisted on the mizzen mast.

Mooring - a permanently anchored ball or buoy to which a boat can be tied.

MSD - marine sanitation device, including toilet, holding tank and connecting lines and valves.

N (November)

Nautical mile - a distance of 6076 feet, equaling one minute of the earth's latitude.

Navigation Rules - laws established to prevent collisions on the water.

No-Go Zone - an area into the wind in which a boat cannot produce power to sail.

Nun - a red, even-numbered buoy, marking the right side of a channel as you return to port. Nuns are usually paired with cans.

O (Oscar)

Offshore wind - wind blowing off (away from) the land.

Offshore - away from or out of sight of land.

Off the wind - sailing downwind.
On the wind - sailing upwind, close-hauled.
Outboard - outside the rail of a boat.
Outhaul - the controlling line attached to the clew of a mainsail used to tension the foot of the sail.
Overpowered - a boat that is heeling too far because it has too much sail up for the amount of wind.
Overtaking - a boat that is catching up to another boat and about to pass it.

P (Papa)
Packing gland - see **stuffing box**.
Painter - the line attached to the bow of a dinghy.
Pan Pan- the internationally recognized distress signal for an urgent situation.
Parallel rulers - two rulers linked and held parallel by hinges.
Pay out - to ease a line.
PFD - abbreviation for a life jacket.
Piling - vertical timber or log driven into the sea bottom to support docks or form a breakwater.
Pinching - sailing too close to the wind.
Pintle - small metal extensions on a rudder that slides into a gudgeon on the transom. The gudgeon/pintle fitting allows the rudder to swing back and forth.
Plot - applying calculations to a chart to determine course or position.
Point - to steer close to the wind.
Points of sail - boat directions in relation to wind direction, i.e., close-hauled, close-reaching, beam reaching, broad reaching, and running.
Port - 1. - the left side of a boat when facing forward. 2. - a harbor. 3. - a window in a cabin on a boat.
Port tack - sailing on any point of sail with the wind coming over the port side of the boat. Also identified as the side opposite the boom.
Prevailing wind - typical or consistent wind conditions.
Propeller - a device, having a revolving hub with radiating blades, which is used for propulsion.
Puff - an increase in wind speed for a short duration.
Pulpit - a stainless steel guardrail at the bow and stern of some boats.
Pushpit - a stainless steel guardrail at the stern of some boats.
Push-pull principle - the explanation of how sails generate power.

Q (Quebec)
Quarter - the sides of the boat near the stern.
Quarter berth - a bunk located under the cockpit.

R (Romeo)
Radar reflector - a metal object with lots of faces at sharp angles which can be spotted by other vessels' radar scopes.
Rail - the outer edges of the deck.
Rake - the angle of the mast.
Range - the alignment of two objects that indicate the middle of a channel.
Raw-water - Water pumped into the engine for cooling.
Reach - one of several points of sail across the wind.
"Ready about" - the command given to the crew to prepare to tack.
"Ready to jibe" - the command given to the crew to prepare to jibe.
Reef - to reduce the size of a sail.
Reefing line - a line used to reduce sail by pulling the lower portion of the sail to the boom.
Reeve - to pass a line through a cringle or block.
Rhumb line - a straight course between two points.
Rig - 1. - the design of a boat's mast(s), standing rigging, and sail plan. 2. - to prepare a boat to go sailing.
Rigging - the wires and lines used to support and control sails.
Right-of-way - the right of the stand-on vessel to hold its course.
Roach - the sail area aft of a straight line running from the head to the clew of a sail.
Rode - line and chain attached from the boat to the anchor.
Roller furling - a mechanical system to roll up a headsail (jib) around the headstay.
Round up - when the boat turns, sometimes abruptly and with a great deal of heel, towards the wind.
Rudder - the underwater fin that is controlled by the tiller or wheel to deflect water and steer the boat.
Run - (point of sail) sailing with the wind coming directly behind the boat.
Running rigging - lines and hardware used to control the sails.

S (Sierra)
Safety harness - strong webbing worn around the chest and attached to the boat to prevent someone from being separated from the boat.
Sail cover - the protective cover used to preserve sails when they are not in use.
Sail ties - pieces of line or webbing used to tie the mainsail to the boom when reefing or storing the sail.
Schooner - a two-masted boat whose foremast is shorter than its mainmast.

APPENDIX

Scope - the ratio of the amount of anchor rode deployed to the distance from the bow to the bottom.

Scull - to propel a boat by swinging the rudder back and forth.

Scupper - cockpit or deck drain.

Seabag - a soft-fabric bag for carrying personal items.

Sea breeze - a wind that blows over the sea and onto the land.

Seacock - a shut off valve to prevent water from entering a thru hull fitting.

Secure - make safe or cleat.

Sécurite- an internationally recognized signal to warn others of a dangerous situation.

Set - 1. the direction of a current. 2. to trim the sails.

Shackle - a metal fitting at the end of a line used to attach the line to a sail or another fitting.

Shake out - to remove a reef and restore the full sail.

Sheave - the rotating wheel inside a block or fitting.

Sheet - the line which is used to control the sail by easing it out or trimming it in.

Shoal - shallow water that may be dangerous.

Shroud - standing rigging at the side of the mast.

Singlehanded - sailing alone.

S-Jibe - the controlled method of jibing with the mainsail crossing the boat under control and the boat's path makes an "S" shaped course.

Skeg - a vertical fin in front of the rudder.

Skipper - the person in charge of the boat.

Slab reefing (jiffy reefing) - lowering and tying off the lower portion of a sail in order to reduce sail area.

Slip - see berth.

Sloop - a single-masted sailboat with mainsail and headsail.

Snub - to hold a line under tension by wrapping it on a winch or cleat.

Sole - the floor in a cockpit or cabin.

Solenoid switch - an electrical switch which shuts off the flow of propane.

Spar - a pole used to attach a sail on a boat, for example, the mast, the boom, a gaff.

Spinnaker - a large billowing headsail used when sailing downwind.

Splice - the joining of two lines together by interweaving their strands.

Spreader - a support strut extending athwartships from the mast used to support the mast and guide the shrouds from the top of the mast to the chainplates.

Spring line - a dockline running forward or aft from the boat to the dock to keep the boat from moving forward or aft.

Squall - a short intense storm with little warning.

Stanchions - stainless steel supports at the edge of the deck which hold the lifelines.

Standing rigging - the permanent rigging (usually wire) of a boat, including the forestay, backstay, and shrouds.

Stand-on vessel - the vessel or boat with the right-of-way.

Starboard - when looking from the stern toward the bow, the right side of the boat.

Starboard tack - sailing on any point of sail with the wind coming over the starboard side of the boat. Also identified as the side opposite the boom.

Stay - a wire support for a mast, part of the standing rigging.

Staysail (STAY-sil) - on a cutter, a second small "inner jib," attached between the bow and the mast.

Stem - the forward tip of the bow.

Step - the area in which the base of the mast fits.

Stern - the aft part of the boat.

Stow - to store properly.

Stuffing box (packing gland) - the opening in the hull where the propeller shaft exits.

Sump - a cavity or tank in the bilge to collect water.

Swamped - filled with water.

T (Tango)

Tack - 1. a course on which the wind comes over one side of the boat, i.e., port tack, starboard tack. 2. - to change direction by turning the bow through the wind. 3. - the lower forward corner of a sail.

Tackle - a sequence of blocks and line that provides a mechanical advantage.

Tail - to hold and pull a line from behind a winch.

Telltales - pieces of yarn or sailcloth material attached to sails which indicate when the sail is properly trimmed.

Throttle - a device for controlling the engine's revolutions per minute (RPM).

Thru-hull - Fittings that pass through the hull to which seacocks and other devices are attached.

Tide - the rise and fall of water level due to the gravitational pull of the sun and moon.

Tiller - a long handle, extending into the cockpit, which directly controls the rudder.

Tiller extension - a handle attached to the tiller which allows the helmsman to sit further out to the side.

Toe rail - a short aluminum or wooden rail around the outer edges of the deck.

Toppinglift - a line used to hold the boom up when the mainsail is lowered or stowed.

Topsides - 1. The sides of the hull between the waterline and the deck. 2. Said of people or objects that are not below. See below.

Transom - the vertical surface of the stern.

Traveler - a track or bridle that controls sideways (athwartships) movement of the mainsail.

Trim - 1. - to pull in on a sheet. 2. - how a sail is set relative to the wind.

Trimaran - a three-hulled sailing vessel.

True wind - the actual speed and direction of the wind when standing still.

Tune - to adjust a boat's standing rigging.

Turnbuckle - a mechanical fitting attached to the lower ends of stays, allowing for the standing rigging to be adjusted.

U (Uniform)

Underway - a vessel is underway when it is not at anchor, not aground, and not made fast to a dock or a mooring.

Unrig - to stow sails and rigging when the boat is not in use.

Upwind - toward the direction of the wind.

USCG - abbreviation for U.S. Coast Guard.

V (Victor)

Vang - see **boom vang**.

Vee-berth - a bunk in the bow of the boat that narrows as it goes forward.

Veer - a clockwise change of wind direction.

Vessel - any sailboat, powerboat or ship.

VHF- abbreviation for Very High Frequency, a two-way radio commonly used for boating.

W (Whiskey)

Wake - waves caused by a boat moving through the water.

Waterline - the horizontal line on the hull of a boat where the water surface should be.

Weather helm - the boat's tendency to head up toward the wind, which occurs when a sailboat is overpowered.

Weather side - see **windward side**.

Whip - to bind together the strands at the end of a line.

Whisker pole - a pole, temporarily mounted between the mast and the clew of a jib, used to hold the jib out and keep it full when sailing downwind.

White caps - waves with foam tops.

Winch - a deck-mounted drum with a handle offering mechanical advantage used to trim sheets. Winches may also be mounted on the mast to assist in raising sails.

Windage - the amount of surface area, including sails, rigging and hull, that's presented to the wind.

Windward - toward the wind.

Windward side - the side of a boat or a sail closest to the wind.

Wing-and-wing - sailing downwind with the jib set on the opposite side of the mainsail.

Working sails - the mainsail and standard jib.

Working sheet - on a sail with two sheets, the sheet tensioned by the wind.

X (X-Ray)

Y (Yankee)

Yawl - a two-masted boat with its mizzen (after) mast shorter than its mainmast and located aft of the rudder post.

Y-valve - a double valve used to redirect water flow.

Z (Zulu)

APPENDIX

INLAND NAVIGATION RULES

NAVIGATION RULES 1-19 — INLAND

PART A — GENERAL

Rule 1 Application

(a) These Rules apply to all vessels upon the inland waters of the United States and to vessels of the United States on the Canadian waters of the Great Lakes to the extent that there is no conflict with Canadian law.

(b)(i) These Rules constitute special rules made by an appropriate authority within the meaning of Rule 1(b) of the International Regulations.

(ii) All vessels complying with the construction and equipment requirements of the International Regulations are considered to be in compliance with these Rules.

(c) Nothing in these Rules shall interfere with the operation of any special rules made by the Secretary of the Navy with respect to additional station or signal lights and shapes or whistle signals for ships of war and vessels proceeding under convoy, or by the Secretary with respect to additional station or signal lights and shapes for fishing vessels engaged in fishing as a fleet. These additional station or signal lights and shapes or whistle signals shall, so far as possible, be such that they cannot be mistaken for any light, shape, or signal authorized elsewhere under these Rules. Notice of such special rules shall be published in the Federal Register and, after the effective date specified in such notice, they shall have effect as if they were part of these Rules.

(d) Traffic separation schemes may be established for the purposes of these Rules. Vessel traffic service regulations may be in effect in certain areas.

(e) Whenever the Secretary determines that a vessel or class of vessels of special construction or purpose cannot comply fully with the provisions of any of these Rules with respect to the number, position, range, or arc of visibility of lights or shapes, as well as to the disposition and characteristics of sound-signalling appliances, the vessel shall comply with such other provisions in regard to the number, position, range, or arc of visibility of lights or shapes, as well as to the disposition and characteristics of sound-signalling appliances, as the Secretary shall have determined to be the closest possible compliance with these Rules. The Secretary may isue a certificate of alternative compliance for a vessel or class of vessels specifying the closest possible compliance with these Rules. The Secretary of the Navy shall make these determinations and isue certificates of alternative compliance for vessels of the Navy.

(f) The Secretary may accept a certificate of alternative compliance isued by a contracting party to the International Regulations if he determines that the alternative compliance standards of the contracting party are substantially the same as those of the United States.

Rule 2 Responsibility

(a) Nothing in these Rules shall exonerate any vessel, or the owner, master, or crew thereof, from the consequences of any neglect to comply with these Rules or of the neglect of any precaution which may be required by the ordinary practice of seamen, or by the special circumstances of the case.

(b) In construing and complying with these Rules due regard shall be had to all dangers of navigation and collision and to any special circumstances, including the limitations of the vessels involved, which may make a departure from these Rules necessary to avoid immediate danger.

Rule 3 General Definitions

For the purpose of these Rules and this Act, except where the context otherwise requires:

(a) The word "vessel" includes every description of water craft, including nondisplacement craft and seaplanes, used or capable of being used as a means of transportation on water;

(b) The term "power-driven vessel" means any vessel propelled by machinery;

(c) The term "sailing vessel" means any vessel under sail provided that propelling machinery, if fitted, is not being used;

(d) The term "vessel engaged in fishing" means any vessel fishing with nets, lines, trawls, or other fishing apparatus which restricts maneuverability, but does not include a vessel fishing with trolling lines or other fishing apparatus which do not restrict maneuverability;

(e) The word "seaplane" includes any aircraft designed to maneuver on the water;

(f) The term "vessel not under command" means a vessel which through some exceptional circumstances is unable to maneuver as required by the Rules and is therefore unable to keep out of the way of another vessel;

(g) The term "vessel restricted in her ability to maneuver" means a vessel which from the nature of her work is restricted in her ability to maneuver as required by these Rules and is therefore unable to keep out of the way of another vessel; vessels restricted in their ability to maneuver include, but are not limited to:

(i) a vessel engaged in laying, servicing, or picking up a navigation mark, submarine cable, or pipeline;

(ii) a vessel engaged in dredging, surveying, or underwater operations;

(iii) a vessel engaged in replenishment or transferring persons, provisions, or cargo while underway;

(iv) a vessel engaged in the launching or recovery of aircraft;

(v) a vessel engaged in mine clearance operations; and

(vi) a vessel engaged in a towing operation such as severely restricts the towing vessel and her tow in their ability to deviate from their course.

(h) The word "underway" means that a vessel is not at anchor, or made fast to the shore, or aground;

(i) The words "length" and "breadth" of a vessel mean her length overall and greatest breadth;

(j) Vessels shall be deemed to be in sight of one another only when one can be observed visually from the other;

(k) The term "restricted visibility" means any condition in which visibility is restricted by fog, mist, falling snow, heavy rainstorms, sandstorms, or any other similar causes;

(l) "Western Rivers" means the Mississippi River, its tributaries, South Pass, and Southwest Pass, to the navigational demarcation lines dividing the high seas from harbors, rivers, and other inland waters of the United States, and the Port Allen-Morgan City Alternate Route, and that part of the Atchafalaya River above its junction with the Port Allen-Morgan City Alternate Route including the Old River and the Red River;

(m) "Great Lakes" means the Great Lakes and their connecting and tributary waters including the Calumet River as far as the Thomas J. O'Brien Lock and Controlling Works (between mile 326 and 327), the Chicago River as far as the east side of the Ashland Avenue Bridge (between mile 321 and 322), and the Saint Lawrence River as far east as the lower exit of Saint Lambert Lock;

(n) "Secretary" means the Secretary of the department in which the Coast Guard is operating;

(o) "Inland Waters" means the navigable waters of the United States shoreward of the navigational demarcation lines dividing the high seas from harbors, rivers, and other inland waters of the United States and the waters of the Great Lakes on the United States side of the International Boundary;

(p) "Inland Rules" or "Rules" mean the Inland Navigational Rules and the annexes thereto, which govern the conduct of vessels and specify the lights, shapes, and sound signals that apply on inland waters; and

(q) "International Regulations" means the International Regulations for Preventing Collisions at Sea, 1972, including annexes currently in force for the United States.

PART B — STEERING AND SAILING RULES

Subpart I — Conduct of Vessels in Any Condition of Visibility

Rule 4 Application

Rules in this subpart apply in any condition of visibility.

Rule 5 Look-out

Every vessel shall at all times maintain a proper look-out by sight and hearing as well as by all available means appropriate in the prevailing circumstances and conditions so as to make a full appraisal of the situation and of the risk of collision.

Rule 6 Safe Speed

Every vessel shall at all times proceed at a safe speed so that she can take proper and effective action to avoid collision and be stopped within a distance appropriate to the prevailing circumstances and conditions.

In determining a safe speed the following factors shall be among those taken into account:

(a) By all vessels:

(i) the state of visibility;

(ii) the traffic density including concentration of fishing vessels or any other vessels;

(iii) the maneuverability of the vessel with special reference to stopping distance and turning ability in the prevailing conditions;

(iv) at night the presence of background light such as from shore lights or from back scatter of her own lights;

(v) the state of wind, sea, and current, and the proximity of navigational hazards;

(vi) the draft in relation to the available depth of water.

(b) Additionally, by vessels with operational radar:

(i) the characteristics, efficiency and limitations of the radar equipment;

(ii) any constraints imposed by the radar range scale in use;

(iii) the effect on radar detection of the sea state, weather, and other sources of interference;

(iv) the possibility that small vessels, ice and other floating objects may not be detected by radar at an adequate range;

(v) the number, location, and movement of vessels detected by radar; and

(vi) the more exact assessment of the visibility that may be possible when radar is used to determine the range of vessels or other objects in the vicinity.

Rule 7 Risk of Collision

(a) Every vessel shall use all available means appropriate to the prevailing circumstances and conditions to determine if risk of collision exists. If there is any doubt such risk shall be deemed to exist.

(b) Proper use shall be made of radar equipment if fitted and operational, including long-range scanning to obtain early warning of risk of collision and radar plotting or equivalent systematic observation of detected objects.

(c) Assumptions shall not be made on the basis of scanty information, especially scanty radar information.

(d) In determining if risk of collision exists the following considerations shall be among those taken into account:

(i) such risk shall be deemed to exist if the compass bearing of an approaching vessel does not appreciably change; and

(ii) such risk may sometimes exist even when an appreciable bearing change is evident, particularly when approaching a very large vessel or a tow or when approaching a vessel at close range.

Rule 8 Action To Avoid Collision

(a) Any action taken to avoid collision shall, if the circumstances of the case admit, be positive, made in ample time and with due regard to the observance of good seamanship.

(b) Any alteration of course or speed to avoid collision shall, if the circumstances of the case admit, be large enough to be readily apparent to another vessel observing visually or by radar; a succession of small alterations of course or speed should be avoided.

(c) If there is sufficient sea room, alteration of course alone may be the most effective action to avoid a close-quarters situation provided that it is made in good time, is substantial and does not result in another close-quarters situation.

(d) Action taken to avoid collision with another vessel shall be such as to result in passing at a safe distance. The effectiveness of the action shall be carefully checked until the other vessel is finally past and clear.

(e) If necessary to avoid collision or allow more time to assess the situation, a vessel shall slacken her speed or take all way off by stopping or reversing her means of propulsion.

(f)(i) A vessel which, by any of these rules, is required not to impede the passage or safe passage of another vessel shall, when required by the circumstances of the case, take early action to allow sufficient sea room for the safe passage of the other vessel.

(ii) A vessel required not to impede the passage or safe passage of another vessel is not relieved of this obligation if approaching the other vessel so as to involve risk of collision and shall, when taking action, have full regard to the action which may be required by the rules of this part.

(iii) A vessel, the passage of which is not to be impeded remains fully obliged to comply with the rules of this part when the two vessels are approaching one another so as to involve risk of collision.

APPENDIX

Rule 9 Narrow Channels

(a)(i) A vessel proceeding along the course of a narrow channel or fairway shall keep as near to the outer limit of the channel or fairway which lies on her starboard side as is safe and practicable.

(ii) Notwithstanding paragraph (a)(i) and Rule 14(a), a power-driven vessel operating in narrow channels or fairways on the Great Lakes, Western Rivers, or waters specified by the Secretary, and proceeding downbound with a following current shall have the right-of-way over an upbound vessel, shall propose the manner and place of passage, and shall initiate the maneuvering signals prescribed by Rule 34(a)(i), as appropriate. The vessel proceeding upbound against the current shall hold as necessary to permit safe passing.

(b) A vessel of less than 20 meters in length or a sailing vessel shall not impede the passage of a vessel that can safely navigate only within a narrow channel or fairway.

(c) A vessel engaged in fishing shall not impede the passage of any other vessel navigating within a narrow channel or fairway.

(d) A vessel shall not cross a narrow channel or fairway if such crossing impedes the passage of a vessel which can safely navigate only within that channel or fairway. The latter vessel shall use the danger signal prescribed in Rule 34(d) if in doubt as to the intention of the crossing vessel.

(e)(i) In a narrow channel or fairway when overtaking, the vessel intending to overtake shall indicate her intention by sounding the appropriate signal prescribed in Rule 34(c) and take steps to permit safe passing. The overtaken vessel, if in agreement, shall sound the same signal. If in doubt she shall sound the danger signal prescribed in Rule 34(d).

(ii) This Rule does not relieve the overtaking vessel of her obligation under Rule 13.

(f) A vessel nearing a bend or an area of a narrow channel or fairway where other vessels may be obscured by an intervening obstruction shall navigate with particular alertness and caution and shall sound the appropriate signal prescribed in Rule 34(e).

(g) Every vessel shall, if the circumstances of the case admit, avoid anchoring in a narrow channel.

Rule 10 Traffic Separation Schemes

(a) This Rule applies to traffic separation schemes and does not relieve any vessel of her obligation under any other rule.

(b) A vessel using a traffic separation scheme shall:

(i) proceed in the appropriate traffic lane in the general direction of traffic flow for that lane;

(ii) so far as practicable keep clear of a traffic separation line or separation zone;

(iii) normally join or leave a traffic lane at the termination of the lane, but when joining or leaving from either side shall do so at as small an angle to the general direction of traffic flow as practicable.

(c) A vessel shall, so far as practicable, avoid crossing traffic lanes but if obliged to do so shall cross on a heading as nearly as practicable at right angles to the general direction of traffic flow.

(d)(i) A vessel shall not use an inshore traffic zone when she can safely use the appropriate traffic lane within the adjacent traffic separation scheme. However, vessels of less than 20 meters in length, sailing vessels and vessels engaged in fishing may use the inshore traffic zone.

(ii) Notwithstanding sub-paragraph (d)(i), a vessel may use an inshore traffic zone when en route to or from a port, offshore installation or structure, pilot station or any other place situated within the inshore traffic zone, or to avoid immediate danger.

(e) A vessel other than a crossing vessel or a vessel joining or leaving a lane shall not normally enter a separation zone or cross a separation line except:

(i) in cases of emergency to avoid immediate danger;

(ii) to engage in fishing within a separation zone.

(f) A vessel navigating in areas near the terminations of traffic separation schemes shall do so with particular caution.

(g) A vessel shall so far as practicable avoid anchoring in a traffic separation scheme or in areas near its terminations.

(h) A vessel not using a traffic separation scheme shall avoid it by as wide a margin as is practicable.

(i) A vessel engaged in fishing shall not impede the passage of any vessel following a traffic lane.

(j) A vessel of less than 20 meters in length or a sailing vessel shall not impede the safe passage of a power-driven vessel following a traffic lane.

(k) A vessel restricted in her ability to maneuver when engaged in an operation for the maintenance of safety of navigation in a traffic separation scheme is exempted from complying with this Rule to the extent necessary to carry out the operation.

(l) A vessel restricted in her ability to maneuver when engaged in an operation for the laying, servicing or picking up of a submarine cable, within a traffic separation scheme, is exempted from complying with this Rule to the extent necessary to carry out the operation.

Subpart II — Conduct of Vessels in Sight of One Another

Rule 11 Application

Rules in this subpart apply to vessels in sight of one another.

Rule 12 Sailing Vessels

(a) When two sailing vessels are approaching one another, so as to involve risk of collision, one of them shall keep out of the way of the other as follows:

(i) when each has the wind on a different side, the vessel which has the wind on the port side shall keep out of the way of the other;

(ii) when both have the wind on the same side, the vessel which is to windward shall keep out of the way of the vessel which is to leeward; and

(iii) if a vessel with the wind on the port side sees a vessel to windward and cannot determine with certainty whether the other vessel has the wind on the port or on the starboard side, she shall keep out of the way of the other.

(b) For the purpose of this Rule the windward side shall be deemed to be the side opposite to that on which the mainsail is carried or, in the case of a square-rigged vessel, the side opposite to that on which the largest fore-and-aft sail is carried.

Rule 13 Overtaking

(a) Notwithstanding anything contained in Rules 4 through 18, any vessel overtaking any other shall keep out of the way of the vessel being overtaken.

(b) A vessel shall be deemed to be overtaking when coming up with another vessel from a direction more than 22.5

degrees abaft her beam; that is, in such a position with reference to the vessel she is overtaking, that at night she would be able to see only the sternlight of that vessel but neither of her sidelights.

(c) When a vessel is in any doubt as to whether she is overtaking another, she shall assume that this is the case and act accordingly.

(d) Any subsequent alteration of the bearing between the two vessels shall not make the overtaking vessel a crossing vessel within the meaning of these Rules or relieve her of the duty of keeping clear of the overtaken vessel until she is finally past and clear.

Rule 14   Head-on Situation

(a) Unless otherwise agreed, when two power-driven vessels are meeting on reciprocal or nearly reciprocal courses so as to involve risk of collision each shall alter her course to starboard so that each shall pass on the port side of the other.

(b) Such a situation shall be deemed to exist when a vessel sees the other ahead or nearly ahead and by night she could see the masthead lights of the other in a line or nearly in a line or both sidelights and by day she observes the corresponding aspect of the other vessel.

(c) When a vessel is in any doubt as to whether such a situation exists she shall assume that it does exist and act accordingly.

(d) Notwithstanding paragraph (a) of this Rule, a power-driven vessel operating on the Great Lakes, Western Rivers, or waters specified by the Secretary, and proceeding downbound with a following current shall have the right-of-way over an upbound vessel, shall propose the manner of passage, and shall initiate the maneuvering signals prescribed by Rule 34(a)(i), as appropriate.

Rule 15   Crossing Situation

(a) When two power-driven vessels are crossing so as to involve risk of collision, the vessel which has the other on her starboard side shall keep out of the way and shall, if the circumstances of the case admit, avoid crossing ahead of the other vessel.

(b) Notwithstanding paragraph (a), on the Great Lakes, Western Rivers, or water specified by the Secretary, a vessel crossing a river shall keep out of the way of a power-driven vessel ascending or descending the river.

Rule 16   Action by Give-Way Vessel

Every vessel which is directed to keep out of the way of another vessel shall, so far as possible, take early and substantial action to keep well clear.

Rule 17   Action by Stand-on Vessel

(a)(i) Where one of two vessels is to keep out of the way, the other shall keep her course and speed.

(ii) The latter vessel may, however, take action to avoid collision by her maneuver alone, as soon as it becomes apparent to her that the vessel required to keep out of the way is not taking appropriate action in compliance with these Rules.

(b) When, from any cause, the vessel required to keep her course and speed finds herself so close that collision cannot be avoided by the action of the give-way vessel alone, she shall take such action as will best aid to avoid collision.

(c) A power-driven vessel which takes action in a crossing situation in accordance with subparagraph (a)(ii) of this Rule to avoid collision with another power-driven vessel shall, if the circumstances of the case admit, not alter course to port for a vessel on her own port side.

(d) This Rule does not relieve the give-way vessel of her obligation to keep out of the way.

Rule 18   Responsibilities Between Vessels

Except where Rules 9, 10, and 13 otherwise require:

(a) A power-driven vessel underway shall keep out of the way of:

(i) a vessel not under command;

(ii) a vessel restricted in her ability to maneuver;

(iii) a vessel engaged in fishing; and

(iv) a sailing vessel.

(b) A sailing vessel underway shall keep out of the way of:

(i) a vessel not under command;

(ii) a vessel restricted in her ability to maneuver; and

(iii) a vessel engaged in fishing.

(c) A vessel engaged in fishing when underway shall, so far as possible, keep out of the way of:

(i) a vessel not under command; and

(ii) a vessel restricted in her ability to maneuver.

(d) A seaplane on the water shall, in general, keep well clear of all vessels and avoid impeding their navigation. In circumstances, however, where risk of collision exists, she shall comply with the Rules of this Part.

Subpart III — Conduct of Vessels in Restricted Visibility

Rule 19   Conduct of Vessels in Restricted Visibility

(a) This Rule applies to vessels not in sight of one another when navigating in or near an area of restricted visibility.

(b) Every vessel shall proceed at a safe speed adapted to the prevailing circumstances and conditions of restricted visibility. A power-driven vessel shall have her engines ready for immediate maneuver.

(c) Every vessel shall have due regard to the prevailing circumstances and conditions of restricted visibility when complying with Rules 4 through 10.

(d) A vessel which detects by radar alone the presence of another vessel shall determine if a close-quarters situation is developing or risk of collision exists. If so, she shall take avoiding action in ample time, provided that when such action consists of an alteration of course, so far as possible the following shall be avoided:

(i) an alteration of course to port for a vessel forward of the beam, other than for a vessel being overtaken; and

(ii) an alteration of course toward a vessel abeam or abaft the beam.

(e) Except where it has been determined that a risk of collision does not exist, every vessel which hears apparently forward of her beam the fog signal of another vessel, or which cannot avoid a close-quarters situation with another vessel forward of her beam, shall reduce her speed to the minimum at which she can be kept on course. She shall if necessary take all her way off and, in any event, navigate with extreme caution until danger of collision is over.

APPENDIX

INTERNATIONAL NAVIGATION RULES

NAVIGATION RULES 1-19 — INTERNATIONAL

PART A — GENERAL

Rule 1 Application

(a) These Rules shall apply to all vessels upon the high seas and in all waters connected therewith navigable by seagoing vessels.

(b) Nothing in these Rules shall interfere with the operation of special rules made by an appropriate authority for roadsteads, harbors, rivers, lakes or inland waterways connected with the high seas and navigable by seagoing vessels. Such special rules shall conform as closely as possible to these rules.

(c) Nothing in these Rules shall interfere with the operation of special rules made by the Government of any State with respect to additional station or signal lights, shapes or whistle signals for ships of war and vessels proceeding under convoy, or with respect to additional station or signal lights or shapes for fishing vessels engaged in fishing as a fleet. These additional station or signal lights, shapes or whistle signals shall, so far as possible, be such that they cannot be mistaken for any light, shape or signal authorized elsewhere under these Rules.

(d) Traffic separation schemes may be adopted by the Organization for the purpose of these Rules.

(e) Whenever the Government concerned shall have determined that a vessel of special construction or purpose cannot comply fully with the provisions of any of these Rules with respect to the number, position, range or arc of visibility of lights or shapes, as well as to the disposition and characteristics of sound-signalling appliances, such vessel shall comply with such other provisions in regard to the number, position, range or arc of visibility of lights or shapes, as well as to the disposition and characteristics of sound-signalling appliances, as her Government shall have determined to be the closest possible compliance with these Rules in respect of that vessel.

Rule 2 Responsibility

(a) Nothing in these Rules shall exonerate any vessel, or the owner, master or crew thereof, from the consequences of any neglect to comply with these Rules or of the neglect of any precaution which may be required by the ordinary practice of seamen, or by the special circumstances of the case.

(b) In construing and complying with these Rules due regard shall be had to all dangers of navigation and collision and to any special circumstances, including the limitations of the vessels involved, which may make a departure from these Rules necessary to avoid immediate danger.

Rule 3 General Definitions

For the purpose of these Rules, except where the context otherwise requires:

(a) The word "vessel" includes every description of water craft, including nondisplacement craft and seaplanes, used or capable of being used as a means of transportation on water.

(b) The term "power-driven vessel" means any vessel propelled by machinery.

(c) The term "sailing vessel" means any vessel under sail provided that propelling machinery, if fitted, is not being used.

(d) The term "vessel engaged in fishing" means any vessel fishing with nets, lines, trawls or other fishing apparatus which restrict maneuverability, but does not include a vessel fishing with trolling lines or other fishing apparatus which do not restrict maneuverability.

(e) The word "seaplane" includes any aircraft designed to maneuver on the water.

(f) The term "vessel not under command" means a vessel which through some exceptional circumstance is unable to maneuver as required by these Rules and is therefore unable to keep out of the way of another vessel.

(g) The term "vessel restricted in her ability to maneuver" means a vessel which from the nature of her work is restricted in her ability to maneuver as required by these Rules and is therefore unable to keep out of the way of another vessel.

The term "vessels restricted in their ability to maneuver" shall include but not be limited to:

(i) a vessel engaged in laying, servicing or picking up a navigation mark, submarine cable or pipeline;

(ii) a vessel engaged in dredging, surveying or underwater operations;

(iii) a vessel engaged in replenishment or transferring persons, provisions or cargo while underway;

(iv) a vessel engaged in the launching or recovery of aircraft;

(v) a vessel engaged in mine clearance operations;

(vi) a vessel engaged in a towing operation such as severely restricts the towing vessel and her tow in their ability to deviate from their course.

(h) The term "vessel constrained by her draft" means a power-driven vessel which, because of her draft in relation to the available depth and width of navigable water is severely restricted in her ability to deviate from the course she is following.

(i) The word "underway" means that a vessel is not at anchor, or made fast to the shore, or aground.

(j) The words "length" and "breadth" of a vessel mean her length overall and greatest breadth.

(k) Vessels shall be deemed to be in sight of one another only when one can be observed visually from the other.

(l) The term "restricted visibility" means any condition in which visibility is restricted by fog, mist, falling snow, heavy rainstorms, sandstorms or any other similar causes.

PART B — STEERING AND SAILING RULES
Section I — Conduct of Vessels in Any Condition of Visibility

Rule 4 Application

Rules in this Section apply to any condition of visibility.

Rule 5 Look-out

Every vessel shall at all times maintain a proper look-out by sight and hearing as well as by all available means appropriate in the prevailing circumstances and conditions so as to make a full appraisal of the situation and of the risk of collision.

Rule 6 Safe Speed

Every vessel shall at all times proceed at a safe speed so that she can take proper and effective action to avoid collision and be stopped within a distance appropriate to the prevailing circumstances and conditions.

In determining a safe speed the following factors shall be among those taken into account:

(a) By all vessels:

(i) the state of visibility;

(ii) the traffic density including concentrations of fishing vessels or any other vessels;

(iii) the maneuverability of the vessel with special reference to stopping distance and turning ability in the prevailing conditions;

(iv) at night the presence of background light such as from shore lights or from back scatter of her own lights;

(v) the state of wind, sea and current, and the proximity of navigational hazards;

(vi) the draft in relation to the available depth of water.

(b) Additionally, by vessels with operational radar:

(i) the characteristics, efficiency and limitations of the radar equipment;

(ii) any constraints imposed by the radar range scale in use;

(iii) the effect on radar detection of the sea state, weather and other sources of interference;

(iv) the possibility that small vessels, ice and other floating objects may not be detected by radar at an adequate range;

(v) the number, location, and movement of vessels detected by radar.

(vi) the more exact assessment of the visibility that may be possible when radar is used to determine the range of vessels or other objects in the vicinity.

Rule 7 Risk of Collision

(a) Every vessel shall use all available means appropriate to the prevailing circumstances and conditions to determine if risk of collision exists. If there is any doubt such risk shall be deemed to exist.

(b) Proper use shall be made of radar equipment if fitted and operational, including long-range scanning to obtain early warning of risk of collision and radar plotting or equivalent systematic observation of detected objects.

(c) Assumptions shall not be made on the basis of scanty information, especially scanty radar information.

(d) In determining if risk of collision exists the following considerations shall be among those taken into account:

(i) such risk shall be deemed to exist if the compass bearing of an approaching vessel does not appreciably change;

(ii) such risk may sometimes exist even when an appreciable bearing change is evident, particularly when approaching a very large vessel or a tow or when approaching a vessel at close range.

Rule 8 Action To Avoid Collision

(a) Any action taken to avoid collision shall, if the circumstances of the case admit, be positive, made in ample time and with due regard to the observance of good seamanship.

(b) Any alteration of course and/or speed to avoid collision shall, if the circumstances of the case admit, be large enough to be readily apparent to another vessel observing visually or by radar; a succession of small alterations of course and/or speed should be avoided.

(c) If there is sufficient sea room, alteration of course alone may be the most effective action to avoid a close-quarters situation provided that it is made in good time, is substantial and does not result in another close-quarters situation.

(d) Action taken to avoid collision with another vessel shall be such as to result in passing at a safe distance. The effectiveness of the action shall be carefully checked until the other vessel is finally past and clear.

(e) If necessary to avoid collision or allow more time to assess the situation, a vessel shall slacken her speed to take all way off by stopping or reversing her means of propulsion.

(f)(i) A vessel which, by any of these rules, is required not to impede the passage or safe passage of another vessel shall, when required by the circumstances of the case, take early action to allow sufficient sea room for the safe passage of the other vessel.

(ii) A vessel required not to impede the passage or safe passage of another vessel is not relieved of this obligation if approaching the other vessel so as to involve risk of collision and shall, when taking action, have full regard to the action which may be required by the rules of this part.

(iii) A vessel, the passage of which is not to be impeded remains fully obliged to comply with the rules of this part when the two vessels are approaching one another so as to involve risk of collision.

Rule 9 Narrow Channels

a) A vessel proceeding along the course of a narrow channel or fairway shall keep as near to the outer limit of the channel or fairway which lies on her starboard side as is safe and practicable.

(b) A vessel of less than 20 meters in length or a sailing vessel shall not impede the passage of a vessel which can safely navigate only within a narrow channel or fairway.

(c) A vessel engaged in fishing shall not impede the passage of any other vessel navigating within a narrow channel or fairway.

(d) A vessel shall not cross a narrow channel or fairway if such crossing impedes the passage of a vessel which can safely navigate only within such channel or fairway. The latter vessel may use the sound signal prescribed in Rule 34(d) if in doubt as to the intention of the crossing vessel.

(e)(i) In a narrow channel or fairway when overtaking can take place only if the vessel to be overtaken has to take action to permit safe passing, the vessel intending to overtake shall indicate her intention by sounding the appropriate signal prescribed in Rule 34(c)(i). The vessel to be overtaken shall, if in agreement, sound the appropriate signal prescribed in Rule 34(c)(ii) and take steps to permit safe passing. If in doubt she may sound the signal prescribed in Rule 34(d).

(ii) This Rule does not relieve the overtaking vessel of her obligation under Rule 13.

(f) A vessel nearing a bend or an area of a narrow channel or fairway where other vessels may be obscured by an intervening obstruction shall navigate with particular alertness and caution and shall sound the appropriate signal prescribed in Rule 34(e).

(g) Any vessel shall, if the circumstances of the case admit, avoid anchoring in a narrow channel.

APPENDIX

Rule 10 Traffic Separation Schemes

(a) This Rule applies to traffic separation schemes adopted by the Organization and does not relieve any vessel of her obligation under any other rule.

(b) A vessel using a traffic separation scheme shall:

(i) proceed in the appropriate traffic lane in the general direction of traffic flow for that lane;

(ii) so far as practicable keep clear of a traffic separation line or separation zone;

(iii) normally join or leave a traffic lane at the termination of the lane, but when joining or leaving from either side shall do so at as small an angle to the general direction of traffic flow as practicable.

(c) A vessel shall, so far as practicable, avoid crossing traffic lanes but if obliged to do so shall cross on a heading as nearly as practicable at right angles to the general direction of traffic flow.

(d)(i) A vessel shall not use an inshore traffic zone when she can safely use the appropriate traffic lane within the adjacent traffic separation scheme. However, vessels of less than 20 meters in length, sailing vessels and vessels engaged in fishing may use the inshore traffic zone.

(ii) Notwithstanding subparagraph (d)(i), a vessel may use an inshore traffic zone when en route to or from a port, off-shore installation or structure, pilot station or any other place situated within the inshore traffic zone, or to avoid immediate danger.

(e) A vessel other than a crossing vessel or a vessel joining or leaving a lane shall not normally enter a separation zone or cross a separation line except:

(i) in cases of emergency to avoid immediate danger;

(ii) to engage in fishing within a separation zone.

(f) A vessel navigating in areas near the terminations of traffic separation schemes shall do so with particular caution.

(g) A vessel shall so far as practicable avoid anchoring in a traffic separation scheme or in areas near its terminations.

(h) A vessel not using a traffic separation scheme shall avoid it by as wide a margin as is practicable.

(i) A vessel engaged in fishing shall not impede the passage of any vessel following a traffic lane.

(j) A vessel of less than 20 meters in length or a sailing vessel shall not impede the safe passage of a power-driven vessel following a traffic lane.

(k) A vessel restricted in her ability to maneuver when engaged in an operation for the maintenance of safety of navigation in a traffic separation scheme is exempted from complying with this Rule to the extent necessary to carry out the operation.

(l) A vessel restricted in her ability to maneuver when engaged in an operation for the laying, servicing or picking up of a submarine cable, within a traffic separation scheme, is exempted from complying with this Rule to the extent necessary to carry out the operation.

Section II — Conduct of Vessels in Sight of One Another

Rule 11 Application

Rules in this Section apply to vessels in sight of one another.

Rule 12 Sailing Vessels

(a) When two sailing vessels are approaching one another, so as to involve risk of collision, one of them shall keep out of the way of the other as follows:

(i) when each has the wind on a different side, the vessel which has the wind on the port side shall keep out of the way of the other;

(ii) when both have the wind on the same side, the vessel which is to windward shall keep out of the way of the vessel which is to leeward;

(iii) if a vessel with the wind on the port side sees a vessel to windward and cannot determine with certainty whether the other vessel has the wind on the port or on the starboard side, she shall keep out of the way of the other.

(b) For the purposes of this Rule the windward side shall be deemed to be the side opposite to that on which the mainsail is carried or, in the case of a square-rigged vessel, the side opposite to that on which the largest fore-and-aft sail is carried.

Rule 13 Overtaking

(a) Notwithstanding anything contained in the Rules of Part B, Sections I and II any vessel overtaking any other shall keep out of the way of the vessel being overtaken.

(b) A vessel shall be deemed to be overtaking when coming up with another vessel from a direction more than 22.5 degrees abaft her beam, that is, in such a position with reference to the vessel she is overtaking, that at night she would be able to see only the sternlight of that vessel but neither of her sidelights.

(c) When a vessel is in any doubt as to whether she is overtaking another, she shall assume that this is the case and act accordingly.

(d) Any subsequent alteration of the bearing between the two vessels shall not make the overtaking vessel a crossing vessel within the meaning of these Rules or relieve her of the duty of keeping clear of the overtaken vessel until she is finally past and clear.

Rule 14 Head-on Situation

(a) When two power-driven vessels are meeting on reciprocal or nearly reciprocal courses so as to involve risk of collision each shall alter her course to starboard so that each shall pass on the port side of the other.

(b) Such a situation shall be deemed to exist when a vessel sees the other ahead or nearly ahead and by night she could see the masthead lights of the other in a line or nearly in a line and/or both sidelights and by day she observes the corresponding aspect of the other vessel.

(c) When a vessel is in any doubt as to whether such a situation exists she shall assume that it does exist and act accordingly.

Rule 15 Crossing Situation

When two power-driven vessels are crossing so as to involve risk of collision, the vessel which has the other on her own starboard side shall keep out of the way and shall, if the circumstances of the case admit, avoid crossing ahead of the other vessel.

Rule 16 Action by Give-way Vessel

Every vessel which is directed to keep out of the way of another vessel shall, so far as possible, take early and substantial action to keep well clear.

Rule 17 Action by Stand-on Vessel

(a)(i) Where one of two vessels is to keep out of the way the other shall keep her course and speed.

(ii) The latter vessel may however take action to avoid collision by her maneuver alone, as soon as it becomes apparent to her that the vessel required to keep out of the way is not taking appropriate action in compliance with these Rules.

(b) When, from any cause, the vessel required to keep her course and speed finds herself so close that collision cannot be avoided by the action of the give-way vessel alone, she shall take such action as will best aid to avoid collision.

(c) A power-driven vessel which takes action in a crossing situation in accordance with subparagraph (a)(ii) of this Rule to avoid collision with another power-driven vessel shall, if the circumstances of the case admit, not alter course to port for a vessel on her own port side.

(d) This Rule does not relieve the give-way vessel of her obligation to keep out of the way.

Rule 18 Responsibilities between Vessels

Except where Rules 9, 10 and 13 otherwise require:

(a) A power-driven vessel underway shall keep out of the way of:

(i) a vessel not under command;

(ii) a vessel restricted in her ability to maneuver;

(iii) a vessel engaged in fishing;

(iv) a sailing vessel.

(b) A sailing vessel underway shall keep out of the way of:

(i) a vessel not under command;

(ii) a vessel restricted in her ability to maneuver;

(iii) a vessel engaged in fishing.

(c) A vessel engaged in fishing when underway shall, so far as possible, keep out of the way of:

(i) a vessel not under command;

(ii) a vessel restricted in her ability to maneuver.

(d)(i) Any vessel other than a vessel not under command or a vessel restricted in her ability to maneuver shall, if the circumstances of the case admit, avoid impeding the safe passage of a vessel constrained by her draft, exhibiting the signals in Rule 28.

(ii) A vessel constrained by her draft shall navigate with particular caution having full regard to her special condition.

(e) A seaplane on the water shall, in general, keep well clear of all vessels and avoid impeding their navigation. In circumstances, however, where risk of collision exists, she shall comply with the Rules of this Part.

Section III — Conduct of Vessels in Restricted Visibility

Rule 19 Conduct of Vessels in Restricted Visibility

(a) This Rule applies to vessels not in sight of one another when navigating in or near an area of restricted visibility.

(b) Every vessel shall proceed at a safe speed adapted to the prevailing circumstances and conditions of restricted visibility. A power-driven vessel shall have her engines ready for immediate maneuver.

(c) Every vessel shall have due regard to the prevailing circumstances and conditions of restricted visibility when complying with the Rules of Section I of this Part.

(d) A vessel which detects by radar alone the presence of another vessel shall determine if a close-quarters situation is developing and/or risk of collision exists. If so, she shall take avoiding action in ample time, provided that when such action consists of an alteration of course, so far as possible the following shall be avoided:

(i) an alteration of course to port for a vessel forward of the beam, other than for a vessel being overtaken;

(ii) an alteration of course toward a vessel abeam or abaft the beam.

(e) Except where it has been determined that a risk of collision does not exist, every vessel which hears apparently forward of her beam the fog signal of another vessel, or which cannot avoid a close-quarters situation with another vessel forward of her beam, shall reduce her speed to the minimum at which she can be kept on her course. She shall if necessary take all her way off and in any event navigate with extreme caution until danger of collision is over.

A complete set of the Navigation Rules, International-Inland (COMDTINST M16672.2B) is available at most marine bookstores, chandleries or the U.S. Government Printing Office: www.access.gpo.gov

US Sailing Basic Cruising Certification

The Basic Cruising graduate will have successfully demonstrated the ability to responsibly skipper and crew an auxiliary powered cruising sailboat, during daylight hours, within sight of land in moderate wind and sea conditions.

Recommended Equipment: It is recommended that Basic Cruising Certification courses and examinations be conducted on 23' to 32' sloop-rigged cruising keelboats with auxiliary power and with adequate equipment inventory to complete all required certification outcomes.

Prerequisite: The prerequisite for Basic Cruising Certification is a US Sailing Basic Keelboat Certification.

Certification Requirements: Basic Cruising Certification requires the successful completion of the following knowledge and skill requirements. These requirements are expected to be able to be performed safely with confident command of the boat in a wind range of 5 to 15 knots. Some regions may have stronger prevailing conditions, which are acceptable if the candidate can safely control the boat, and be aware of his or her limitations in these conditions. The certified candidate will be able to skipper a keelboat up to 32' in length.

Practical Skills
Preparation to Sail:
1. Demonstrate ability to recognize and forecast prevailing local weather conditions.
2. Perform an inspection of running rigging, standing rigging and hull integrity.
3. Check the inventory, location and operation of required safety equipment.
4. Check the auxiliary power systems (as applicable to your boat): location and operation of engine controls, engine mechanical and fluids check, transmission controls, ventilation system and cooling system.
5. Check the electrical system (as applicable to your boat): main battery switch, electrical control panel and battery terminals.
6. Check the bilge pump system (as applicable to your boat): operation of manual and electrical pumps, intake maintenance and bilge pump alarms.
7. Check the head systems (as applicable to your boat): location of controls, equipment operation, holding tanks and proper setting of valves.

8. Check the fresh water system (as applicable to your boat): adequate quantity, operation of manual and electrical pumps, and proper setting of valves.
9. Check the anchoring system (as applicable to your boat): anchors, shackles, rodes, chafing equipment and windlass.
10. Check all other equipment specific to your boat not indicated above.

Crew Operations and Skills:
11. Demonstrate winch operation and the proper procedures for clearing a fouled winch.
12. Demonstrate tying and use of knots: clove hitch, sheet bend and rolling hitch. Review stopper knot, bowline, cleat hitch, round turn & two half hitches and square knot.
13. Demonstrate how to heave a line.
14. Demonstrate the use of sail controls: halyards, sheets, traveler, cunningham/downhaul, outhaul, adjustable backstay (if applicable), boom vang, leech lines, jib fairleads and boom toppinglift.
15. Demonstrate the operation of a VHF radio: operation of controls, channel usage, call sign, weather channels and simulate an emergency call.
16. Demonstrate a comprehensive crew briefing and plan of responsibilities.

Leaving the Dock or Mooring:
17. Demonstrate appropriate helmsman and crew coordination and skills for departure under power suitable to the conditions: line handling, casting off, fending off and boathandling.
18. Demonstrate the use of docklines, including springlines, for boat control while departing.
19. Demonstrate stowing of docklines and fenders.

Boat Control in Confined Waters:
20. Demonstrate in close quarters under power: speed and momentum control, windage and prop walk control, and command of the crew.
21. Demonstrate ability to maneuver under sail in close quarters: short tacking and controlled jibes.
22. Demonstrate a recovery plan for an engine failure in a crowded and busy harbor.

Navigation:
23. Determine your position in open water, the position of your destination, your intended track and approximate travel time to that destination.
24. Confirm your progress along that intended track with visual observations or with visual observations and electronic confirmation. Obtain and utilize relevant tide and current information. Using a chart, verify sufficient depth for a planned cruise.

Boat Control in Open Water:

25. Demonstrate ability to steer a compass course with changes in course to a given destination.
26. Demonstrate helm and boat control in a variety of wind and sea conditions.

Heavy Weather Sailing:

27. Demonstrate proper reefing techniques: determining when to reef, roller furling or changing headsails, reefing the mainsail, dropping sails, shaking out a reef, and rehoisting underway.
28. Demonstrate helm and boat control while sailing under shortened sail.

Overboard Rescue Methods:

29. Properly demonstrate one of the overboard rescue methods, which is most appropriate for: your sailing ability, boat type, crew experience, wind and sea conditions, and maintaining constant visual contact with the person in water.

Safety and Emergency Procedures:

30. Simulate procedure and operation of VHF radio in various emergency situations.
31. Simulate failure of steering system, and demonstrate steering and boat control with sails.

Anchoring Techniques:

32. Select an anchorage, and demonstrate appropriate helmsman and crew coordination and skills for properly anchoring with a single anchor under power.
33. Demonstrate appropriate helmsman and crew coordination and skills for retrieving your anchor under power.

Returning to the Dock or Mooring:

34. Demonstrate appropriate helmsman and crew coordination and skills for arrival under power suitable to the conditions: boathandling, deploying fenders, stopping and tying up.
35. Demonstrate correct use and deployment of docklines, including springlines.

Securing the Boat Properly:

36. Demonstrate stowing of sails, rigging and equipment. Thoroughly clean the boat, and install any covers and dock power equipment.
37. Check both the electrical and bilge systems for dock operation.
38. Check the locks on companionway, lockers and hatches. Make a final check of docklines, spring lines and fender placement.

Knowledge

Crew Operations and Skills:

1. Describe typical crew responsibilities and communications while aboard an auxiliary powered cruising sailboat.
2. Explain weather recognition and forecasting techniques for a day sail.
3. Explain the sequence for determining blocked engine cooling system circulation.
4. Understand the different types and operation of stoves, and fuel systems.
5. Be familiar with the use of a float plan.
6. Understand your state and local boating regulations.

Sailing Theory:

7. Describe sailboat dynamics: Center of Effort, Center of Lateral Resistance, and effects and influences of lee and weather helm.
8. Describe real and apparent wind, and their relationship to each other.

Leaving the Dock or Mooring:

9. Understand the effects of wind, tide and currents in relation to the boat and surrounding area, while preparing to get underway.
10. Describe the differences and alternatives for leaving under power in upwind, crosswind and downwind situations.

Navigation:

11. Understand the organization of a Mercator chart, including: latitude and longitude, chart scales, chart symbols (Chart No.1), title block, warnings, how to determine distance and direction, the relationship between time/speed/distance.
12. Understand the U.S. aids to navigations (IALA System B).
13. Understand the magnetic influences that may disrupt compass readings.
14. Understand variation and describe the use of a compass rose.
15. Understand Digital Selective Calling (DSC) and Maritime Mobile Service Identity (MMSI).

Navigation Rules, International-Inland:

16. Know the Navigation Rules, International-Inland, Rules 4 through 10 for steering and sailing.
17. Describe the Navigation Rules, International-Inland, for Stand-On and Give-Way sailboats and powerboats for collision avoidance and understand your state and local boating regulations.

Boat Control in Open Water:

18. Explain the dangers of a lee shore.

APPENDIX

Overboard Rescue Methods:

19. Understand the Quick-Stop, Lifesling-type, and Figure-8 overboard rescue methods under sail to include: constant visual contact with the person in water, communications, rescue plan, sequence of maneuvers, boathandling, course sailed, pickup approach and coming alongside the person in water (or simulated object).

20. Describe methods of getting a person in water back on deck after the vessel is stopped alongside.

21. Explain when overboard recovery should be done under power and the inherent dangers.

Safety and Emergency Procedures:

22. Describe recovery methods after going aground.

23. Be familiar with firefighting equipment on board: regulations, types, location and operation.

24. Be familiar with the location and operation of emergency steering system and boat control during failure of the steering system.

25. Understand towing techniques: maneuvering onto a tow, handling and securing a towline, chafing protection, boat speed, dropping off a tow and communications.

26. Describe the proper function of lifelines and pulpits.

27. Explain proper fueling techniques and potential hazards.

28. Explain the purpose and use of a radar reflector.

29. Be familiar with the U.S. Coast Guard safety requirements for auxiliary powered vessels.

30. Be familiar with at least six distress or emergency signals.

Anchoring Techniques:

31. Explain different types of anchors and various bottom conditions suited for each type.

32. Explain how to determine the required scope of an anchor rode.

33. Describe accepted etiquette when anchoring in the vicinity of other boats.

Returning to the Dock or Mooring:

34. Describe the differences and alternatives for arrival under power in upwind, crosswind and downwind situations.

US Sailing and your sport.

Since 1897 the United States Sailing Association (US Sailing) has provided support for American sailors at all levels of sailing — in all kinds of sailboats. The primary objective of its Training Program is to provide a national standard of quality instruction for all people learning to sail. The US Sailing Keelboat Certification System includes a series of books such as *Basic Cruising*, a program of student certifications and an extensive educational and training program for instructors. It is one of the most highly developed and effective national training systems for students and sailing instructors and is recognized nationally and internationally.

US Sailing is a non-profit organization and the official National Governing Body of Sailing as designated by the U. S. Congress in the Amateur Sports Act. It has a national Training Program for sailors in dinghies, windsurfers, multihulls and keelboats. It is also the official representative to World Sailing.

The US Sailing Keelboat Certification System is designed to develop safe, responsible and confident sailors who meet specific performance and knowledge standards. (See US Sailing Basic Cruising Certification on page 123 for the Basic Cruising standards.) There are other benefits for you as well. You can start at the Basic Keelboat certification level and progress through Basic Cruising, Bareboat Cruising, Coastal Navigation, and even go on to Coastal Passage Making, Celestial Navigation and Offshore Passage Making.

With your US Sailing certifications and experience documented in the *Official Logbook*, you will have a passport to cruising and chartering boats locally or nationally.

Basic Cruising is intended as a supplement to your sailing lessons, rather than as a substitute for them. It was created to help you accelerate your learning curve and clarify your understanding of the concepts and techniques of sailing and cruising.

What Makes Sailing Special?
The sport of sailing is open to people of all ages, incomes and abilities. Sailing offers virtually limitless choices of boats, each with its own unique characteristics, and the opportunity to explore an adjacent cove or an exotic tropical location.

Most sailors will acquire entry-level skills quite rapidly. Mastering those skills is an experience that will be rewarding, exciting and pleasurable for a lifetime.

As you continue to sail, you will find that sailing is more than simply being pushed and pulled by the wind. For most people, sailing is meeting new friends, enjoying nature's beauty and challenge, and sharing a unique fellowship with all boaters. A tremendous camaraderie exists among sailors, particularly on the water, which makes sailing — and the people who do it — very special.

What can US Sailing do for you?

US Sailing is committed to helping you discover and enjoy the beauty, relaxation, challenge and friendships of sailing. As part of this commitment we offer:

THE KEELBOAT CERTIFICATION SYSTEM with its various levels of training and certification:

Basic Keelboat. To responsibly skipper and crew a simple daysailing keelboat in familiar waters in light to moderate wind and sea conditions.

Basic Cruising. To responsibly skipper and crew an auxiliary powered cruising sailboat during daylight hours within sight of land in moderate wind and sea conditions.

Bareboat Cruising. To responsibly skipper, crew or bareboat charter an inboard auxiliary powered cruising sailboat within sight of land to a port or an anchorage during daylight hours in moderate to strong wind and sea conditions.

Coastal Navigation. To properly use traditional navigation techniques and electronic navigation for near coastal passage making.

Coastal Passage Making. To responsibly skipper and crew an inboard auxiliary powered cruising sailboat for coastal or offshore passages in strong to heavy conditions, including zero visibility and nighttime, in unfamiliar waters out of sight of land.

Celestial Navigation. To navigate using celestial techniques and integrating celestial with traditional navigation techniques.

Offshore Passage Making. To responsibly skipper and crew an inboard auxiliary powered cruising sailboat to any destination worldwide.

THE SMALL BOAT CERTIFICATION SYSTEM which is available for dinghy, daysailer and multihull sailors in two wind speed ranges: light and heavy air.

Plus many other useful services:

US Sailing certified instructors help you achieve new skills and knowledge using up to date and safe methods.

Course materials, including this book, presented in a highly visual format to help you gain competency and confidence in your sailing skills and knowledge.

The Official Logbook, recognized nationally and internationally, to document your US Sailing certifications and experience when chartering boats nationally.

A website of accredited US Sailing schools, that use US Sailing certified instructors and US Sailing course materials. www.sailingcertification.com

US Sailing Safety-at-Sea seminars.

Racing Rules and handicap rating systems.

US Sailing membership makes you a part of the National Governing Body for the Sport of Sailing as well as giving you discounts on products and services that US Sailing offers. **www.ussailing.org**